Thinking Teaching

Thinking Teaching

Stories, Insights, and Strategies to Ignite Reflection, Discussion, and Imagination

NANCY LYNNE WESTFIELD

CASCADE *Books* • Eugene, Oregon

THINKING TEACHING
Stories, Insights, and Strategies to Ignite Reflection, Discussion, and Imagination

Cascade Books
An Imprint of Wipf and Stock Publishers
199 W. 8th Ave., Suite 3
Eugene, OR 97401

www.wipfandstock.com

PAPERBACK ISBN: 979-8-3852-6033-1
HARDCOVER ISBN: 979-8-3852-6034-8
EBOOK ISBN: 979-8-3852-6035-5

Cataloguing-in-Publication data:

Names: Westfield, Nancy Lynne, author.

Title: Thinking teaching : stories, insights, and strategies to ignite reflection, discussion, and imagination / Nancy Lynne Westfield.

Description: Eugene, OR: Cascade Books, 2026. | Includes index.

Identifiers: ISBN 979-8-3852-6033-1 (paperback). | ISBN 979-8-3852-6034-8 (hardcover). | ISBN 979-8-3852-6035-5 (ebook).

LCSH: Theology—Study and teaching. | Religion—Study and teaching. | College teaching.

Classification: BV4020 W43 2026 (print). | BV4020 (epub).

VERSION NUMBER 04/13/26

Our world yearns for the creative work of those who understand the liberating power of education. This book is in celebration of the brave souls and dedicated colleagues who dare to teach imaginatively, with authenticity and grace.

Together, let us learn to be free.

Contents

Introduction

PURPOSE OF THE BOOK

Like all crafts worth pursuing, teaching must be nurtured, cultivated, refined if it is to deepen and be continually impactful. Regardless of the season of your career, your teaching can be improved upon. Let me invite you into a conversation about teaching with the intent of enhancing your expertise—reenforcing essentials, challenging complacency, inspiring new ideas, and encouraging creativity with reliance upon wisdom. Teaching, after all, is a human encounter fraught with the promise of possibility and opportunity.

Many of us have reoccurring questions about our professions as scholars, especially the dimensions of teaching and the teaching life. Even more, we wonder if we are making a difference. We are afraid our efforts are undervalued, and our energies are squandered.

Many of us are tired, others hopeful. Some of us are fulfilled, some running on empty. Most of us feel an enthusiasm for learning and teaching—the mutuality with our students is exciting and life-giving—even if those enthusiasms are diminished by our institutions. We see insight, commitment, and action being born in students and this gives us vitality. The work yearned for by our souls finds satisfaction in interactions with students. We like being a part of a learning environment—even those with problems. Our passion for teaching still finds its expression. Yet, we wonder how our commitments to an academic discipline will have bearing upon the wider world through our teaching. In short, our commitment to teaching is complicated.

Students surprise us. Their worlds are often so different from ours. They are asking perennial questions about meaning making, justice, and living a fulfilled life. Our adult learners want the ability to thrive in their vocations, and to be able to support their families and their obligations. We are surprised by our students' experiences and concerns. We wonder how we connect with them and are dismayed when we do not. We wonder about the significance of our syllabi and teaching practices. We fret over the grading process. We remember when we were students and realize those days are gone.

We work with our colleagues to fulfill the commitments of a learning community. We hear our colleagues speak about their concerns for teaching, students, and the life of our institution. Together we build curricula. We intend to teach in ways that are rich and meaningful, yet too often we are too pressed or too scared to take any time to reflect on our teaching with others. Too often grind culture gets the best of us. The dysfunctions in our departments and schools keep getting in the way of our collective work as a faculty. We seek conversation that will enable, empower, and support us.

This book offers you space to think about your own teaching and invites you to join with others in "thinking teaching." These storied essays lean heavily upon my experiences and reflections from my own classroom adventures and teaching life. Over the many years, I have worked hard at my teaching. I love the time I spent as a faculty colleague teaching and learning in classrooms. My hope is that the essays will bolster you and foster new energies within you.

The short essays are drawn from my blogs posted from 2015 to 2025 on the Wabash Center for Teaching and Learning in Religion and Theology. As such, some refer to key communal events during that time—political elections, the COVID pandemic along with the pandemics of racism and economic disparity, the increase in the hire of contingency colleagues on faculties, the expansion of shrinking and closing schools, global phenomenon. My intent is that my essays will assist you in reflecting upon your own time and place and through your own lenses. As you read, think about your own teaching and teaching life, the context of your work, the adults who are your students, then reflect alone or with a group of colleagues.

This resource provides succinct essays focused upon the identities of teachers, the essentials of teaching, ways classroom experiences might better meet the adult learner, and new approaches to imagining learning activities, assignments, and the teaching life. The storied essays are organized by these conversation areas: teachers, the students, classes, practices, schools, and next steps. The reflections invite teachers to look at themselves, the effect of teaching on their own lives as well as their souls, and their hopes for the future. I think of this book as a creative and engaged way to work on improving teaching.

INVITATION TO ACTIVE REFLECTION

Thinking Teaching is an invitation. I am inviting you to a space of reflection, imagination, and new considerations to strengthen your classrooms. These reflections can be useful as a personal reflection tool or, equally, can be useful for group conversation. The goal of critical and imaginative reflection is to cause you to think about your own identity, hopes, dreams, aspirations, and new ways of making the teaching profession more impactful in the lives of students.

Consider making use of the book in these ways:

- Personal Reflection—Journaling
  - Choose any of the essays.
  - Think about what the reflection stimulates in you. What images, stories, memories, and questions does it draw from you?
  - Review the reflection at the end of each entry. See which ones draw your attention.
  - Consider your own teaching. Think about your institutional context.
  - As you compare your thoughts about the essay and your practices, see what insights you gain.
  - Keep a journal of your ideas, responses, and reactions as you work your way through the entire book. Your insights will be valuable.
- Group Reflection—Small Group or Entire Faculty
  - Gather with a group of colleagues.
  - Read the reflections. You may want to gather weekly or monthly to review many or all of the reflections.
  - Ask what ideas, concerns, and commitments the essay calls forth in you.
  - Examine the reflection questions in each essay and choose one or two to engage.

- Compare reactions and experiences with one another.
- Think about ways to help each other to improve teaching and learning.
- Plan for changes in your teaching, course designs, and curriculum.

REPRESENTING MY FAMILY

Many of these essays are written in first person and tell stories of my family, my friends, and my loved ones. In these stories we hear the wisdom of my family. I was born into a family of teachers. We are people who believe that education is a way for African Americans, and all people, to find liberation and to practice freedom. I have worked seriously at taking this emancipatory sensibility and virtue into my work as a scholar of religion, i.e., education is meant to lift people up, engender creativity, coax generativity, and heal the soul. I hope I have, with this spirit, well represented my family in my classrooms and in this writing. My obligation to teach and to teach well is part of my legacy. As you read *Thinking Teaching*, I hope you remember your family, teachers, and friends without whose teaching and care the opportunity to teach would not be yours. I hope this resource serves to rekindle your passions for teaching.

PART ONE

Teachers—We Teach Who We Are

Who is the self who teaches? What is my profession as a teacher? In what ways do I name and claim this identity? What differences do I hope to make? As I teach, is my soul enlivened and nurtured? In what ways do I renew myself for teaching?

1

Articulating Your Intellectual Project

As teachers, you must have and be able to articulate your intellectual project. It is good if it happens in the early stages of your scholarly career, but it is never too late.

A scholar's intellectual project is:

- the ever-present cornerstone of the scholarly career;
- the fifty-thousand-foot/big-picture pursuit of their intellectual work;
- the grounding of your philosophical pursuit;
- the perennial question, the persistent issue;
- the quest;
- the epistemological guiding-star for decision-making;
- the scholarly passion;
- intellectual haunting; and
- that which captures your curiosity, interests, imaginations, and thirsts—regardless of status or season of our career.

Your intellectual project is why you wanted to be a scholar and why you continue in scholarship.

There will always be smaller, contributory ventures which engage, address, and actualize your central inquiry or question, BUT those smaller schemes are never the whole of your intellectual project. They may satisfy an aspect or element of your intellectual aspiration. However, the desire of your intellectual inquiry is bigger, much bigger, than any one expression created as a single book, journal article, course offering, or artistic rendering.

The key is to be able to articulate the most basic description of your intellectual project. This is a necessity for your scholarship and to participate in a scholarly community. Your intellectual project, over the course of your career, and over the seasons of your work, will refine and deepen. Your project might even shift and change. Regardless of any changes and shifts, your articulation of your principal project is paramount. You must be able to say what you are about in a way that is pithy, accessible, and personable.

An intellectual project is not:

- a single job or even your entire career; on the contrary, your places of employment are in service to your project.
- a single grant proposal, committee accomplishment, single publication or panel participation.
- defined by your approaches to your scholarship; the methodologies of engagement for research, teaching, or writing are not the project.
- dependent upon, nor redundant to, the conversation in your academic field; your project is meant to add to the conversation already in the field.

Your intellectual project is distinctively your own.

You need a boiler plate speech.

Your project must be articulable in three to seven sentences. You should have a succinct paragraph that describes, in its most elegant form, your intellectual project. This is as much for your own comfort and focus as for those who ask you about your work. Knowing your project, as well as being able to concisely communicate your project, allows you to work your project.

This work of articulation is not easy. Your intellectual project's articulation might feel elusive or vague. Intellectual projects can be bold, "in your face," dazzling. They can also be coy, temperamental, and evasive. Knowing your project is good—being able to articulate your project is the goal. Articulation may take time and great effort.

How do you know what your intellectual project is? Questions to consider:

- What is your curiosity? Or to what are you compelled? To what are you called?
- What are your perennial questions? What are your big, philosophical, epistemological questions that are worth spending a career or lifetime pursuing?
- What issues would you study/explore/interrogate/pursue with or without salary?
- What agenda do you bring to every job?
- Toward what questions or issues do you bend every job, all writing, and all your courses?
- What has broken your heart, and so now, to mend your heart, what will your scholarship be about?
- What is your immortal wound, and how are you saving your own life through scholarly pursuit?
- What, for a lifetime, will you resist, protest, contest, and fight against? What wrong will you right? What makes you so mad that you spring into action—especially the action of intellectual work and scholarly labor?
- What is your vision for the new world, and how will this vision be embodied by your scholarship?
- At the end of your life, when you look back over your long and illustrative career, to what did you say yes?
- What is the pattern of your yes-saying, and what can you glean as having been your project?
- Who is your inspiration and what was/is their project? How will you attach to it, fulfill it?
- What is the intersection of your gifts/talents with the mighty needs of the world?
- Why did your people send you to school? For them, what will be your scholarly accomplishment and contribution? How will your scholarship liberate your people?

Consider that your intellectual project is likely very vivid to other people. Ask someone who knows you and your work. What do they believe your project is?

Going through a search process routinely helps with clarifying your intellectual passion, scholarly focus, and intent. These processes force you to articulate your vision, perspective, aspirations, and scholarly itches. Consider applying for a job and see what happens with articulating your intellectual project.

Consider the following to assist with coming to know and articulate your project:

- Write and rewrite an intellectual mission statement, write an elevator speech, write in simple prose, three to seven sentences; practice those sentences on family, friends, and colleagues until they make sense to them and have resonance with you.
- In question format, create a list of fifty to one hundred questions that frame your curiosity and pursuits, then cull the list down to the questions you want to pursue for years to come.
- In poetic or in creative forms, design a rendition of your intellectual project, then contemplate it; after contemplation, write your paragraph.
- If your scholarly project is woven into a course, assign students the task of mapping, charting, postering, or displaying the basic concepts of the course. This allows you to see what you talk about when you talk about what you talk about. Often your students know your work of thinking better than you do.
- Invite several faculty colleagues to create public or digital displays of their own intellectual projects, then host a gathering to explore and celebrate the current and future work of the colleagues.
- Plan several recorded conversations with a trusted colleague who will dialogue with you as you think through, think out loud, and articulate.
- Reread your dissertation. Use that as a springboard to say what you are actually about.

FOR REFLECTION . . .

1. How does your intellectual project affect your teaching?
2. How does your intellectual project affect your commitments, interact with those projects of your colleagues, support the mission of the school?
3. How does your intellectual project nurture you?

2

What If Learning Is Miraculous?

I DO NOT BELIEVE TEACHING itself to be miraculous. Yet, I can bear witness to miracles that have come with teaching. The wonders come in the learning. Learning is both improbable and extraordinary.

Classrooms with adult learners can be places where the splendor of miracles is known.

The first kind of miracle depends upon time. On the first day of the course, students racked with hesitation, reticence, nervousness, fear of failure, and fear of success are the same students who miraculously enter the classroom on the final day of class with confidence, sometimes swagger, having metabolized that which they previously did not know. Time can afford us miracles if we can see the shifts, modifications, accepted considerations, and the full-out rethink. Sometimes, over the span of a few semesters, or in between the first session and the last, through learning activities, discussions, cognitive dissonance, the yearning for wisdom, the torment of grappling with new ideas, and the challenge of grasping new practices, skills, and habits, students learn that the world is more than they previously suspected or feared.

The second miracle happens when the illusion of inferiority is successfully shattered. Teaching is an embodied art. I inhabit any classroom as I am. I am, by the pronouncement of my physical body, an African American, woman, age sixty plus. By US societal norms created by white supremacy, capitalism, patriarchy, misogyny, misogynoir, and racism, I am perceived as inferior. I am, according to the accepted (albeit contested by some) systemic hatreds that permeate social norms, at the bottom of the societal and academy hierarchy. I am, as an older Black woman, less than those who are men, those who are white, and those who are young. The politics of inferiority is operational in society, and these real and dangerous mindsets enter my classrooms in the imaginations of my students. Inferiority is not scientific, but it is a real part of the moral matrix of US society and US cultural imagination. It is reality. Regardless of my credentials or standing in the academic community, my students have been given license by ruling power structures to see me as inferior. The miracle is when I can dissuade students—Black, white, and otherwise—that the lie of inferiority must be exorcised, purged, eliminated in and beyond my classroom. Too many times, I have been unsuccessful in provoking this miracle—it is not an easy miracle to summon. But there have been a few times—I can bear witness. There have been a few students who have left my courses no longer deceived or duped by patriarchal mindsets. They discover the ability to refuse to live in, and believe in, a narrow world of sameness and homogeneity. They muster the capacity to see a world that is dripping with Maybe? and Perhaps?

This is their miracle: They have had the audacity to accept the keys that unlock their miseducated minds.

The third miracle is the hardest to perform and not easily witnessed or claimed. It is the miracle of possibility. It is akin to the miracle of ridding students of white supremacy but not exactly the same. Students, especially adult students, insist upon risk-less learning. They want assurances, guarantees—proof. They prefer learning experiences to being like Disney World simulations—no risk and only gleeful reward. A championing of mediocrity. They want learning that is carefully scripted, with an ending that is foolproof and predictable. With experience, I have learned to watch for the glad surprise in my teaching. It is in the surprise, the unplanned for and sometimes unpleasant, that we have a chance of being visited by new possibility, new opportunity, and perhaps grace. Some semesters, everything happens as planned on cue and with exacted precision. These are the semesters I know the learning is insubstantial or empty. Other semesters, the unplanned for provides much needed astonishment.

Beyond these three kinds of classroom miracles, my hunch is that the best miracles happen when I can—simply and with a Buddhist's kind of detachment—invite students to take from my teaching what they can.

Keep in mind that the successful completion of assignments, the fulfillment of student learning outcomes, and the granting of high grades does not necessarily indicate the activity of the miraculous.

FOR REFLECTION . . .

1. By the end of your long and productive teaching career, what miracles will you have performed or witnessed? What miracles, between now and retirement, will you invoke, provoke, evoke in your classrooms or in your teaching life?
2. If one of the tools of teaching is the ability to rely upon, ascertain, identify, or produce miracles, what habits, practices, or strategies will you need to nurture to strengthen this capacity?
3. When you were a student, what miracles assisted your learning and sustained your knowledges?
4. Ask yourself and trusted colleagues to recall or recount a particular classroom miracle or two. Then consider how these experiences have reenforced your vocation and helped you claim your identity as a teacher.

3

Exercising Professional Agency

A SUMMER JOY OF the Wabash Center is hosting workshop groups on our campus. The visits allow me to have conversations with participants over breakfast, or chats while visiting the local ice cream shop. A significant concern for our early career colleagues has to do with agency—or the lack thereof.

Colleagues will recount an incident, then ask, What to do when pressed upon by senior colleagues or administrators? What to say when overtaxed by committee assignments? What to say upon hire? What to do when bullied by colleagues? What to do when confused or disoriented about institutional protocols? What to say when the culture of the institution is not clearly defined or when the interpretation of the faculty handbook is unclear? WHAT TO DO? WHAT TO SAY?

When I hear their stories, feel their anxiety and reticence, I advise them that there is a solution for this dilemma. I encourage them that they need to develop, nurture, practice, and understand agency. A formulaic or recipe-ed response to a specific difficulty would be foolish or ill conceived. Without being part of the context and without having a clear vantage of the situation, I do not know the better/best answer to their contextual question. I do know that in many of these situations, what is needed by the colleague is a gesture of professional agency.

In the world of academia, we must have agency for ourselves and for our own intellectual projects. Some of the conversations have revealed that colleagues are mis-defining or mis-characterizing agency. Demonstrating professional agency is not:

- asserting unmerited or unjust privilege;
- being demanding, aggressive, or mean-spirited;
- a gesture showing a lack of humility;
- a request to squander institutional resources;
- a wheedling of anger;
- a stepping beyond rank or role;
- being uppity and not knowing your place;
- a lack of cooperation;
- a lack of participation;
- an inability to get along;
- an admission of not belonging;
- an admission of frailty or lack; or
- a showing of ill-preparedness.

Simply put, habits and practices of agency are about knowing what you want and what you need for your own flourishing and for the benefit of your institution, then working toward those needs and wants. Gestures of agency are meant to increase the likelihood of communal respect, dignity, and career success.

Exercising agency is engaging the wherewithal to pursue purposeful action and pursue goals free from the threat of violence, retribution, or retaliation. Acts of agency begin in the hiring process, continue while forging relationships with colleagues, and work to create healthy patterns of communication.

We all need the skills of agency.

Complex organizations have opportunities and challenges for which the exercise of agency is required to make full use of the opportunities and navigate the challenges. All colleges, universities, and seminaries have their own organizational maze of complexity. Learning to read the context, adapt and understand the context requires agency, savvy, and wherewithal to be confident.

It is too easy to give your agency away. Nothing good comes to the employee or to the institution when employees give agency away.

Schools who are grappling with issues, habits, and practices of diversity, equity, inclusion, and belonging sometimes falter when non-white colleagues exercise agency for themselves or for their own intellectual projects. BIPOC colleagues, often newly hired faculty in predominantly white institutions, struggle with the fear of retribution. We learn not to exercise agency for fear of being thought ungrateful for the job or being thought unfit for scholarship. We develop a kind of "go along to get along" mentality. This collegial stifling is detrimental to the faculty.

Negotiation is key to exercising agency. Abilities of negotiation take self-knowledge; demand a professional plan; require clarity about the role and responsibility you want now and in the future. You must read your context to understand how the institution functions formally and informally. Learning to read your context is as important as learning to have agency.

Yes, there are dangers in some contexts. There are stories of retaliation and punishment for speaking up and for advocating for yourself. If you are working in a climate that would retaliate against an early-career colleague for asking for professional development or for requesting support for research—perhaps that is not the post for you. You have options.

When I was a tenure-track scholar, I began to have casual conversations with a senior colleague about the unmet curricular needs of African American students. Together, he and I began to imagine a new project to strengthen the curriculum. Mid-way through our dreaming, I abruptly interrupted our conversation. I said to my colleague that this project could not happen because he and I had no funding. He smirked. He assured me that funding would not be an issue. What I did not know at the time was that my colleague had, at a time, been one of the school's deans. He knew the school had several under-tapped, restricted funds, designated for student support. In a few weeks, he and I presented the dean with a written proposal and accompanying budget. To my surprise and delight, the dean funded our idea—using funds from restricted accounts. Our project ran for many years.

I am not saying that all schools have under-tapped funds for projects or that deans will fund internal proposals. I am suggesting that new and needed ideas, with the agency of collaborating colleagues, can create projects that will benefit the students and assist with career goals and aspirations.

Learning to exercise agency, negotiate, read the context, and have clarity about professional aspirations and plans takes time and intention. In this case, experience is the best teacher. It also takes assistance from trusted colleagues.

FOR REFLECTION . . .

1. Create a map or outline that shows your planned road to tenure, promotion, or contract renewal. Include in your map or outline those activities, accomplishments, work products, and items in your portfolio that are required for your advancement.
2. Add a timeline to your map. Decide if there are points of negotiation that would benefit you or the institution.
3. Reflect upon and strategize about ways of strengthening the many aspects of your work, then ask what kind of agency is needed to fulfill that plan.
4. Consider showing a colleague your map and talk about what is possible, in your context, to reinforce your work efforts. There are likely opportunities for which you are uninformed.
5. Negotiate for what is needed to fulfill your plan.

4

Knowing Your Place

THOSE OF US SERVING on faculties cannot escape the deep influence of the culture of the school upon our scholarship. Where you teach has as much to do with your scholarly formation as what you teach. The location of the doing of your scholarship will allow or deny your sense of belonging, rootedness, and contribution. For this reason, we must develop a curiosity for our context and an imagination for elsewhere. Ask yourself: What is this place to me? What has this place been for those like me? Is there a healthier place for me and my work?

In the early years of my career, participation in Wabash Center afforded me conversations on scholarly identity and formation for which my place of employment did not know how to provide. The lack of mentoring I received from my school was in no way unique. They were not neglectful. I have come to understand that few schools in higher education provide in-depth, intentional faculty formation. Wabash Center programming, then and now, fills a gap for networking and provides opportunities for critical reflection and planning. We provide exposure for faculty to the varieties of pedagogical approaches and dialogue for ways of achieving those approaches. These conversations are often life-giving and career-saving. Routinely, Wabash Center provides a space to prepare you for knowing your place.

Faculty are taught the importance of learning to read the context in which they are employed. We dissuade colleagues from thinking that the performance of, and achievements in, scholarship can be thought of as being generic or universal. No two schools are the same. All schools have known procedures as well as unspoken expectations, whispered secrets, and under-tapped resources.

I remember it clearly. It was an assignment that substantially impacted my career. The assignment given to the cohort group was to:

- compile all the institutional documents to which you are privy (e.g., faculty handout, tenure process and procedure instructions, promotion process, school mission statement, organizational chart, statement of charter, history, accreditation report(s), strategic plan, etc.);
- read all the compiled documents and take notes as you read; and
- considering your school context, create a map/plan of your
    - (1) teaching, (2) service, and (3) scholarship for one year, three years, five years, seven years.

We were instructed to return to next summer's gathering with a thoughtful plan for our own scholarship in our own contexts.

I tell you confessionally, but not ashamedly, that if I had not been given this assignment at Wabash, I would not have made an intentional study of my location, nor would I have created a clear path for my scholarship. Fulfilling this assignment gave me insights that I did not know I needed.

When I compiled and read the university materials, I gained knowledge of the place that I had not previously known and that had not been made clear to me. Creating my map lowered my anxiety about the tenure process. The exercise made me more articulate about who I was as a scholar, and what I wanted for myself in my scholarly pursuits. My aspirations became vivid. It was a kind of liberation.

And so, more than twenty years later, I am instructing our associate directors to develop a map, a plan, a schedule that reflects and actualizes their aspirations and hopes for their own scholarship. They cannot, must not, wait for me to shape them into my image. Their scholarly identity must be in their own hands and hearts. They will have to decide if rooting their work in the place of Wabash Center satisfies the need of their soul. Here are the nine reflection questions I offered to them:

- What does it mean to understand your work as scholarship?
    - What, for you, is the production of new knowledge?
    - What does it mean to see yourself as a scholar of religion?
- How does your family make sense of your profession?

    - ¤ How does your community make sense of this profession?
    - ¤ What do you imagine to be the advantages and disadvantages of your career for your loved ones?
    - ¤ How will you keep connected to your family as you do this work?

- Thinking in metaphors or similes, what scholarly identity are you imagining and pursuing?
- Since scholarship is typically organized and judged in activities of teaching, service, and research/publication, how will you pursue each of these elements? Be specific.
    - ¤ Are there other scholarly pursuits beyond these three elements that are of interest (e.g., activism, entrepreneurship)?
- What expressions of scholarship, or discrete projects, do you want to pursue in the next two years, five years, ten years?
    - ¤ How do these projects fit into the institutional narrative and mission? What are the obstacles to these pursuits?
- Who are your scholarly conversation partners? Who are your mentors?
- What is your scholarly niche, specialty, focus, expertise, and how does this specialty align with your institutional context?
- What will it take for your flourishing? What are the prerequisites for your healing? What are the needed habits and practices to support your scholarly aspirations and plans?
- How do you nurture your imagination, creativity, and artistry?

Be mindful that a plan is meant to guide and not to constrain. Plans will change as new opportunities are recognized and as your context ebbs and flows.

Be mindful that the place that prefers scholars who are indifferent or passive about their own formation will likely object to your exercise of agency and self-determination.

Be mindful that few can call the academy home—so most are strangers in this strange land.

Healthy formation in academic places requires forethought, provisions, anticipation, and time. We must have our own best interests at heart lest we be tossed and entangled by others' agendas for our ideas, our labors, our souls.

FOR REFLECTION . . .

1. Answer the nine questions above.
2. How do you hope you can amend, support, or redirect your energies in the next one to two years?
3. Sit with a mentor and discuss your responses.

5

Teaching While Grieving

My mother was deeply loved. She and my father came to live with me in 2008. Mom and Dad became known in the school community as they regularly attended chapel services, lectures, and community dinners. Students who were my research assistants and teaching assistants were invited to dinner by my mom who still cooked dinner for our family. When invited by the dean, Mom and Dad attended one faculty meeting (Sweet Jesus!! A story for another time!).

My mother, Nancy Bullock Westfield, died on December 7, 2010. We funeralized her in the chapel of Seminary Hall. Many students and colleagues attended the service. I felt an outpouring of love for my family. Mom's homegoing service was a celebration of her life well lived. The celebration highlighted Mom's eighty-one years of service, artistry, nurture, and audacious acts of justice on behalf of poor children and Black children in Philadelphia. And the homegoing, like so many funerals, was the beginning of my family's long walk through grieving our beloved.

In the spring semester of 2011, I was teaching my introductory course. Amy, a brilliant doctoral student, was my teaching assistant. One day while class was convening, Amy, with reticence, asked if she could talk with me in the hallway. I had divided the students into small groups with reflection questions, so the class was, at this moment, on task. I said yes, let's talk now. Amy looked untypically pensive as we walked into the hallway and away from the possibility of our conversation being overheard by our students.

Amy said, "Dr. Westfield . . ." (full pause, and holding her breath). "Umm . . ." (empty pause, and still holding her breath).

Concerned, I asked, "Amy, what is it?"

Amy said, "Dr. Westfield . . ." (taking a breath to gain courage). "Dr. Westfield, you've given that assignment before" (looking me in the eye for the first time).

I did not understand what Amy meant; I frowned to express my puzzlement. My thoughts raced in preparation to disagree. In nanoseconds, I recalled the week before, but I could not recall the learning activities. I turned a half-pivot away from her and looked into the distance as I tried to remember, tried to think. Amy, in a gentle, low tone, said, "Last week you divided the students into conversation groups and gave the same reflection questions."

My immediate reaction was to be defensive and tell her that she was mistaken, but before speaking I looked at her eyes filled with such empathy that I knew she was trying to be helpful. My pause created space for her to speak again, "Remember . . . last week you gave the same assignment . . . and then the students reported in."

"Actually . . . ," Amy went on, "this is the third time you have asked them to reflect upon these questions." As she said these words, I began to remember. I began to orient myself. I began to realize that, indeed, this was the third time I had given the same assignment for class discussion. Without allowing my body to flinch, I jolted from the realization.

In exasperation and embarrassment, I whispered in a quiet and defeated tone, "Amy."

With a warm smile, Amy said, "It's okay—the class understands you're grieving."

Amy and I returned to the classroom, and I called the class out of their small groups. When we gathered, I apologized without giving a reason for the thrice redundant learning activity. I quickly reminded them of the assignment that was due next week, asked for any questions, then dismissed the class about thirty minutes earlier than our scheduled dismissal.

Walking with my mother through her illness and then to her death had been one of the most difficult journeys I have ever taken. Even so, I underestimated the power of sorrow and the ways it can (and does) affect all aspects of life—even the teaching life. My mother's death had taken a toll on me. Thankfully, Amy had my back.

Who is the self who teaches? In happenstances of loss, the self who teaches can become seized by sorrow, hurt, and anguished. Teachers can be people who are grieving. Under these circumstances, teaching as usual is not possible!

In recollecting this classroom experience I am not trying to be confessional—as if I had done something wrong. Rather, I tell the story to convey that grieving necessitates additional support and care. Even the most seasoned and conscientious teacher, while grieving, needs help. I am appreciative to Amy for pointing out that I was stuck. Had she not told me, my realization would have been much more painful and embarrassing. Or worse yet, I would not have ever realized. In teaching while grieving, who has your back? Who is your brave Amy?

For individuals who are in touch with their grief, what grief counselor, spiritual director, or therapist will you engage? For learning communities who possess a depth of communal awareness and a sense of togetherness, what rituals, rites, and conversations will you design for the communal events of loss? What blues songs will you compose? What lamentation will you paint, sculpt, write, create? What new habits will you acquire to honor the dead and the dying? In what ways will you take your grieving and be inspired, be made brave, be summoned to a deeper, more meaningful call of teaching? What new insights on teaching will you incorporate that were inspired in your time and loss and anguish?

Perhaps there will be new ceremonies for graduations, commencements, and baccalaureates? Maybe new liturgies or rites of passage will be included in the senior send-offs, the spring dances, and the yearbooks? Perhaps you will begin or end each class with a moment of silence or of music, or ask students to plan a community-wide protest as a course assignment?

Sometimes grief prevents reflection, prevents action—only affords paralysis. Sometimes while we are grieving all we can do is the little bit we can do; one day at a time. Perhaps, simply keep a journal on your teaching until the grief subsides enough to reflect and plan for change.

The courses I taught in the spring of 2011 were not my best, but they were the best I had to offer at the time. I hope that the little bits I had to offer my students were enough.

Thank you, Amy, for your care and support.

FOR REFLECTION . . .

1. Think about a moment when your grieving affected your teaching and your classroom. Note how you felt. Did the moment make you feel more real, more vulnerable, or too vulnerable and exposed?
2. In what ways did your experience connect with or draw forth experiences of students?
3. Note how your grief shifted your interaction with the content of the class.

6

A Call for Agency

The task is impossible, yet ours to accomplish. Our students need us to shape our classrooms for a future we cannot foresee or anticipate. In the courses we design, our students need us to hone their voices, imaginations, and problem-solving abilities for a future that is unmappable yet will require their navigational skills for survival of our families, neighborhoods, and nation. The world powers are shifting before our very eyes, and we must teach to prepare our students for this change.

A call for agency is not a call to act out or act up. Agency has more to do with activating the responsibilities and powers that came with faculty hire when we joined an institution with a commitment to mission. We are bound to the promise of educating—come what may.

Typically, the mission of the school has to do with educating for the moment at hand, and with an eye toward the coming future. Faculty, as stewards of knowledge production, have a professional obligation to adapt, pivot, adjust so that education remains future minded—especially in a moment when the future will not look like the past. We are teaching in a moment when we do not have the luxury of thinking that adhering to established traditions will save schools or educate our people in the next fifty years. While we need those with agency to guide us into the new possibilities, the new approaches, the new sensibilities of education, too many school contexts have punished, jettisoned, or abandoned those with agency.

Agency, or lack thereof, is one of the perennial themes discussed in gatherings of early career colleagues at Wabash Center. Colleagues invariably bring to the discussion their fears, misinformation, unarticulated needs, desires, and hopes. They disclose their disappointment and misgivings about institutional citizenship and the lack of ownership they feel for their own professional duties. When asked by the workshop leaders why they feel so disregarded, they say:

- "I assumed that my needs are just like everyone else's. They [the administration] should know what I need without me asking."
- "I don't ask questions in meetings because I do not want to appear stupid."
- "I don't like to ask too many questions because I am new."
- "I really think someone else knows the curriculum better than I do, so I leave it up to the senior scholars."
- "I have decided to wait until I am [tenured, promoted, finished with my book]—THEN I will start speaking up about the workings of the school."
- "I do not want to ask for a faculty handbook because they might think I am causing trouble."
- "When colleagues ask me to lunch, I say no. I don't want the department head to think I am colluding with them."
- "I say yes to every extra assignment. I don't want colleagues to think I am unavailable or lazy."
- "I don't make use of the teaching center. I don't want my colleagues to think I do not know how to teach."
- "My only mentor is my dissertation advisor who retired three years ago. I do not want colleagues to think I need advice."
- "I am going to pitch my idea for a new class after Dr. XXXX retires in two years."
- "I do not vote in faculty meetings because I do not want colleagues to think I take sides."
- "I wanted to say something, but I did not know how the colleagues would react."

These are the kinds of responses given by the fearful and the distracted. The lack of agency signals that there is a denial of authority, an abdication of responsibility, a giving away of power, a squandering of opportunity. As some of the most educated people on the planet we are asking permission to do the jobs for which we are depended upon. My fear is that now, in this crisis, we are incapable of shaping our classrooms for the unknown future—we might be, as my father would say, "a day late and a dollar short." As educators, we are in a reckoning moment when we must take agency if our craft of teaching is to be relevant and worthwhile.

Moving forward, we know that higher education will need to imagine, invigorate, and conjure up new schools as well as establish new approaches for entire systems of education. Professional timidity will sabotage these efforts. Faculty colleagues who have no agency, no forthrightness, no vision for the new, and who refuse or are unable to take authority for the job will only serve to further compromise the system and foreclose the freedom and creativity needed now and in the future. Leadership that is flexible, resilient, imaginative, and willing to convene open dialogue and struggle with challenging questions is what is needed as we press onward through the fog!

FOR REFLECTION . . .

1. What are the obstacles to your own agency?
2. How has your agency grown with the seasons of your career?
3. What is at stake should your leadership go unvoiced?
4. Who are your conversation partners for discussing this moment of crisis and the ways it is affecting teaching?
5. Where are the open dialogues that address the new possibilities for the coming future?

7

Bring Forth Voice

One of my favorite reality TV shows is *Project Runway.* It is a contest of fashion designers who compete by designing new garments each week. Each episode the designers receive a new design challenge. The episode ends with renowned fashion designers judging the garments made by the contestants, then eliminating the weakest design. While I know the producers control the storyline of each episode, my fascination is in watching the ways the contestants grapple with the challenges of design, of being creative, of being human, of problem solving.

Watching artists create a new garment in the context of a challenge intrigues me as I think about the work of teaching and learning to bring forth the voice.

A favorite episode involved a most difficult challenge. The designers were instructed to create a garment based upon some aspect of New York City—the aspect of the city was of their own choosing—the contestants were led to believe that this was the entire challenge. They were given time to sketch, then were taken to the fabric store to purchase fabrics. Once they got back to the workroom a twist was added to the challenge. The designers were instructed to switch their bags of fabric with another designer. In other words, they had to create a garment using the fabric another designer had selected. This unexpected twist sent the designers reeling! The camera vividly showed the designers in shock, in panic, in fear. Emotional turmoil seized the group. The usually chatty, noisy, electric work room was still, and the mood was somber. Some designers became angry and railed and cussed. Others cried. One designer was so stymied she considered dropping out of the competition because the fabric she was given was unfamiliar to her and not to her taste. Further into the episode the designers, in multiple ways, rallied to the challenge. The designers struggled and found unanticipated ways to solve the problems of the challenge. Many expanded their repertoire of design. They found new solutions. By the runway show—all designers had garments to show. The judges commented that so many of the pieces looked new and fresh compared to previous weeks' work. The judges praised the group of designers for solving the problem well and with a refreshing aesthetic. Design is problem solving.

Cultural aesthetics are not generic nor universal. Cultural aesthetics are determined by solving problems in particular contexts and arriving at solutions that have political implications and aesthetic qualities. If we have the eye to see, we will recognize that we are surrounded by, immersed in, design. Our coffee pots and mugs are designed. Computer keyboards are designed, then redesigned. Our national and international transportation systems (on the grandest scale) are designed. From the smallest detail of life to the meta-patterns of society—design choices are made by us, and for us the design of a building portrays the architect's philosophy. Visible, as well as experienced while walking through the building, is the architect's beliefs about the nature of humanity. The viewpoint of the architect is expressed in the use of sunlight, the means and methods of access, the places of privacy, and the materials that construct the walls, floors, and doorknobs. The use of line, space, color, contrast (value), form, texture, and space translates his/her understanding of human bodies and the ways we work, play, and live in community. Architects become known for their "look"—their style, their aesthetic opinion, and viewpoints. Even as laypersons, we recognize the work of Frank Lloyd Wright, I. M. Pei, and Leonardo da Vinci. The same could be said about the work of many kinds of designers. In fashion, the aesthetics of Jason Wu, Betsy Johnson, and Donna Karen are easily recognized. In dance, the choreography (design) of Alvin Ailey, Judith Jamison, Katherine Dunham, and Robert Battle are revered. To push the notion of design into sports—the genius of Venus and Serena Williams as designers on the tennis court is renowned the world over.

Design expresses the voice. The voice evolves, matures, and refines throughout the lifetime of the designer. Designers find, summon, and bring forth new answers to old problems over their years of work. The longer they design, the more they discover, uncover, and become aware of new expressions from their own point of view. The more they express their point of view, the more their opinion sharpens and hones. Designers interpret and reinterpret their truths searching for ways to say to the world what they are thinking, feeling, knowing, becoming, and believing. Victor Wooten, Grammy Award–winning jazz musician, says it like this: "An instrument laid on the ground makes no sound. It is the musician who must bring Music forth, or not."[1]

What if, just as the philosophy of the architect is revealed in the blueprints and in the building, the voice of the teacher is revealed in the syllabus and classroom experience? What if, as teachers, we think of ourselves as designers?

What if, in creating our syllabi and planning our teaching lessons, we considered the line, space, color, contrast, form, texture, and space of the course and classroom dynamics—not as whimsy, folly, but with the intent of expressing our genuine voice as critically reflective teachers?

Since design is problem solving, we cannot trivialize this work by saying our students are the problem; that would be like a painter saying the easel and canvas are the problem. Nor can we say the topic at hand is the problem.

Teacher/designers, like all designers, know that the problem to be solved is one of expressing the authentic voice of the teacher and inspiring the authentic voice of the student. In the words of Professor Nel Morton, our task is to "hear each other into speech."[2]

The metric of good teaching is not figuring out a formula for the classroom, then inflicting that formula upon students for an entire teaching career. Designers are after something more than the routine or the generic. Design sensibilities invite teachers to avoid teaching that is tantamount to fast food meals or paint-by-number kits. They challenge teachers to avoid teaching that is sterile and tasteless. Designers and artists invite new thinking and learning experiences to make the learning sticky, lasting, participatory, and beautiful.

Suppose you were to take out a large, ample sampling of your syllabi, then arrange them chronologically. Spread them out on the floor (or the computer screen). Look for the ways your teaching voice has matured, evolved, shifted, and become more refined. What does your voice taste like, sound like, look like, feel like, smell like in the classroom? What is the line,

1. Wooten, *Music Lesson*, 1.

2. Morton, *Journey Is Home*, 205.

space, color, contrast (value), form, texture, and space of your teaching? If you cannot answer these questions, ask your students—they know.

No one is born able to articulate their authentic selves. No one is born knowing their voice or design aesthetic. No one comes into the world knowing how to teach. It takes years to craft and refine your authentic voice—it evolves through work, rehearsal, practice, mistakes, and achievements. Recognizing our individual and collective power to get another person to express themselves freely is the insight toward freedom for both teacher and learner.

FOR REFLECTION . . .

1. Consider your "voice." Note that it is built out of your cultural experiences, your training, your passions as a scholar and teacher, and the support colleagues, family, and friends have given you. Draw a picture of how your voice feels to you. Or paint or use play dough. Find a graphic way to depict your own voice for yourself and for your consideration.
2. Make a list of four or five ways you embody your voice in the classroom. Then make a list of possible ways to improve your embodiment of your own voice.
3. Consider your class preparation—how might your routine and habits be reconsidered to bring forth your voice?

8

Aspiring to Power, Influence, and Humility

One of the first requests I received in my new role as director of the Wabash Center was to convene a group of "late-career" scholars. I said no. The friend requesting the workshop explained that they had participated in an early-career workshop, then a mid-career workshop. So, explained the colleague, it only stands to reason that, now, Wabash Center should host a late-career workshop. I said no. My rationale was that if late-career colleagues knew the richness of the workshop experience, then they should write a proposal and convene a group for one another. Now, in year five of this job, I have received the same earnest appeal many times from other colleagues of my generation. To each request, I have said no—until this past February.

In February, over lunch in Trippet Hall, two colleagues carefully explained to me why Wabash Center needed to support late-career colleagues with a workshop. I listened. Somehow, I was persuaded by this encounter. I have begun to think about the possibility of convening the old(er) colleagues.

In my wondering about this possible gathering, it quickly dawned on me that we have no meaningful name for "late-career" scholars. In the current system, being hired to a faculty position, moving through the tenure-track process, and/or promotion connotes early-career.

The years after tenure and promotion connote mid-career. During the mid-career years some colleagues are promoted to full professor. Many colleagues remain associate professors for the rest of their career. Remaining an associate professor is not an indication of poor scholarship or poor collegiality. I do not like the terms "junior scholar" and "senior scholar" for the contrived and implied assumptions of authority and influence. Emeriti status occurs after retirement. With that said, what is the name of the vocational territory between mid-career and retirement? Why have we not identified this moment in our careers with a significant name that denotes the power of this season and so we can be aspirational? What if during this season of our career we are the best of ourselves and have the most to offer?

I began to think that "late(r)-career" colleagues need a description or profile. So far, here is my profile: We would focus upon a gathering of senior scholars who know they are at their career's apex. We would gather those who have been in the enterprise long enough to know what they know, including their limits. Those with an earned confidence would be invited. These colleagues are no longer ruled by their fears. They are comfortable in their own skin and in their own classrooms. They no longer feel responsible for supporting the status quo. They have a freedom in their professional life that other, younger, less experienced colleagues are not afforded or have not earned. They have garnered enough institutional goodwill and cachet that they are able to take institutional risks—make good trouble—without fear of reprisal or retaliation. They recognize that depression, family obligations, financial challenges, health issues, and creative deserts have not had the last word. They have clear paths, practices, and habits for their generativity in teaching, research, and discovery. They understand the teaching life as, paradoxically, contemplative and publicly active.

They possess a feeling of being on the verge, which is exhilarating. They acknowledge and affirm the late season of their career, their success, who they have become, and the public journey they have undertaken. They are not narcissistic nor are they self-deprecating. Yet, they make time for early-career colleagues as a significant part of their scholarly duties. They are imaginative in their ways of mentoring, advising, counseling, coaching, advocating, allying, and befriending younger colleagues.

The truth is that even if we do not have a name for these people, we all know one or two of these folks. When I was an early-career colleague, several of these folks saved my life—more than once.

These people are powerful and knowledgeable and keep the community sane, somewhat healthy, and mission focused. These are the colleagues who have resisted becoming mean or embittered or simply checking out of faculty life while still cashing the paycheck. These are the colleagues who save us from the bullies, the devils, and those who would haze us, even after tenure. They teach us with their actions how to not act entitled but be service-focused and humble.

There should be a clear path to this season of a career. Early-career colleagues should be aware of the power in this season. I have played with the following names:

- Elder scholars—for too many people the term "elder" connotes being elderly.
- Apex scholars—reminds people of being an apex predator!
- Apogee scholars—nobody other than physics professors get this reference.
- Sherpa scholars—has a kind of symbolism and resonance to the wider meaning of the aforementioned profile but lacks grit.
- Baobab scholars—makes use of the idea of gathering under the baobab tree for wise counsel with elders in the African village, but do enough people know the tree?
- Synergy scholars—communicates that the work is about collaboration, interaction, and cooperation, but it sounds foreign to teachers of religion and theology.

I am still working to name this season of our careers.

FOR REFLECTION . . .

1. As an early-career colleague, what will you do to aspire to this season? If you are in this peer group, what will you do to move into connection with colleagues who are playing these roles and taking on these responsibilities?
2. If you are retired, how will you support those still in the struggle?
3. If you are an administrator, how will you recognize and celebrate the great work these folks provide in your school and for our colleagues?
4. As a late-career scholar, think about how your vocation as a teacher has had many twists, turns, and unexpected happenings. What has surprised you? Over the last five years, what has enlivened your teaching? What has kept you fresh throughout the arc of your career?

9

Dare to Be Amateur at Something

My editor is one of my most ardent supporters and a beloved friend. We are working together on my next book. He has not, in many months, received any pages from me. At a recent gathering, he asked me if I had been writing.

My editor's question was not intended as chastisement nor judgment. His tone of voice was casual, even pleasant. Immediately upon hearing his question, I felt a pang of shame or guilt or embarrassment—one of those kinds of stomach feelings that confirm that you are doing something irresponsible or questionable or inappropriate. Thankfully, my stomach relaxed as quickly as it had tightened. I told him I had not been writing. My editor waited for the explanation or the details. I told him that in the last few months, the time I had previously devoted to writing is now being used for coloring. I expected him to be surprised, but instead he was quizzical.

He asked me what I liked about coloring. I really didn't have an answer—I had not reflected on "why" I liked it. Again, my stomach flinched as if I was childish/shy—pointlessly confessional. I realized that while I am greatly enjoying my newfound hobby, I question my time being spent in this way—especially if it means that I am not writing. Then he said (knowing me and my ways)—it's probably meditative. I accepted his speculation, then I told him I wanted him to look through my coloring books, select the best pieces. I wanted to display my best pieces in my house. He agreed.

Coloring has become my new jam! But I am cautious, timid . . .

The impulse to color was strong during the quarantine, but I resisted it. At that time, the activity seemed frivolous and lacking in enough "productive merit" to warrant pursuit. Then in January of this year, a roundtable participant gifted me a coloring book and colored pencils. During that meeting I began to color. Since that meeting, coloring has become a major pastime. My hesitancy is that I still question my use of time for this enjoyable activity.

When I color, I lose myself. It is a way to relax, enjoy the moment. I focus without concern or worry. When I color there is no cynicism or irony. There is no pursuit. I am not prey. The worries, sorrows, and nameless fears dissipate. While I know these merits and I need these moments, I still question my time being used in this way.

In recent months, I have explored varieties of implements: pencils, pens, gels, glitters, and markers. I now have opinions about fine lines, thick lines, and double-sided utensils. Last week, while grocery shopping, I swung past the back-to-school display to see if there were any markers or colored pencils I was unacquainted with or any refills I might make use of. I made a purchase.

My fascination with this newfound hobby is multifaceted. I am captured by learning to work with color (itself). I am intrigued by the many tints, tones, hues, and shades of any one color, while also being annoyed that for our limited eyesight there are only a few colors in our spectrum. Yes, white and black provide a bit more variability, but not much. I have a very wide lexicon for the color green. I am getting more acquainted with red.

I have learned that the more acquainted I am with a particular subject or object, the more detailed in my coloring of it. This is why I know green. I am a long-time gardener. I have deep knowledge of trees, flowers, vegetables, bees, birds, soils, rocks, and weather. I noticed that when I color a forest scene or landscape a kind of intimate knowing comes into play. I have clarity for the colors I select and the mood I create. When realistic precision is not the aim, I enjoy coloring geometric shapes and patterns. In these pages there are no preconceived ideas of how things "should" look. The freedom of coloring without rules or prescriptions is refreshing.

So many of my administrative duties are managing, planning, supporting, and caring. We set goals, know our aims, and reflect upon our experiences. The hours I spend coloring are hours devoted to creating beauty without the incumbrance of metrics or the obligation of accomplishment. Surely, this is, indeed, time well spent?

Several years ago, I was a participant in a mid-career workshop that provided us the opportunity to develop an art or a craft. During conversation about which art or craft each participant might pursue, the discussions grew tense. As colleagues considered their project options, they became stressed and felt pressed upon. There were tears. After too much discussion, consternation, and push-back, our wise leader, Dr. Willie Jennings, said,

> Everything you put your mind to does not have to be at the highest echelon. You can do something on an amateur level. You can engage in something for the simple pleasure of enjoying it. You can learn something or relearn something without pressuring yourself to be the best at it. You can play at something without becoming an expert at it. Pick an artistic expression that will bring you joy.

This lesson stays with me. This is why I color.

I have not stopped writing. I have started coloring. Right now, expressing ideas in colors feels better than expressing myself in words. I suspect the words will soon return. I hope the colors never depart.

FOR REFLECTION . . .

1. In your life, to keep yourself refreshed and balanced, what is your play? What is your fanciful expression?
2. Note two or three ways you play that give your teaching life vitality and generativity.
3. If you do not already, schedule your practice(s) of play and whimsy on your calendar with as much commitment as you schedule your work.

10

Emotional Labor of Teaching

If I have learned anything in this life of teaching, it is this: The emotional labor of teaching is genuine. Routinely, class sessions left me exhausted. The emotional labor of teaching occurs due to the full engagement of body, mind, spirit, guts, wit, intuition, intellect, and humor, all summoned in the teaching encounter. The depletion was never from a lecture, but from the intensity of conversation with students. Regularly I would need to sit in silence for an hour to regain my energies or have a meal to replenish my body.

When we do our teaching work well, classroom conversation can be powerfully interactive—for students and for us. Teaching religion, in confessional or nonconfessional institutions, can stir up cultural tensions, stretch personal beliefs, raise consciousness, and reenforce ethical obligations. Classrooms where the pursuit of truth is passionate, enthusiastic, and exciting can take an emotional toll on the teachers because of the emotional investment in the endeavor. Interactions with students are often fulfilling but never neutral. The intensity of the conversation when students are expressing curiosity, thinking deeply, connecting previously disconnected ideas, and experiencing new insights can tax our emotional reservoirs.

Emotional labor in the classroom is not a flaw, nor a side effect. Teachers who extend themselves, make themselves available, open their hearts to students must realize that emotional presence—from delight to disappointment—is part of work. Regardless of the season in one's career, navigating identity, belief, and culture without falling into advocacy or detachment is hard work. Vulnerability can be costly.

For those of us who must contend with the disrespect, disregard, and indignity foisted upon us by students who judge us as inferior due to our gender, race, nationality, age, or physical ability, the emotional toll assumes the jagged dimensions of discrimination and injustice. Classroom spaces riddled with unfair bias can be debilitating.

To further complicate the challenge, students' habit of coaxing teachers into boundary-blurring or insisting upon role overload can be aggravating. As an African American woman, students would treat me like women in their families or in their churches. Too often I was relegated to the status of deaconess, mother of the church, pastor's wife, auntie, or favorite cousin. Students, because of their lack of familiarity with an African American woman as a professor, and to appease their nervousness, would think of me as their counselor, lover, therapist, or friend. Many students would signal that I was like a familiar TV character—Florence Johnston, Oprah Winfrey, Aunt Viv, or Clair Huxtable. I refused this status. I rejected the blurring and projection of these roles. I was their teacher. Being a teacher is a status, a role, and an obligation worthy of pursuit and needs no appendages, additions, or attachments.

The emotional labor needs to be monitored, nurtured, and attended to. Over long periods of time, the labor can erode us. Burnout, disengagement, cynicism, ill health, or depression must be avoided. Here are some strategies I have learned over the many years.

PRACTICAL STRATEGIES

1. Practice grounding rituals
   - meditate and pray before class to center yourself
   - start class with breathing or meditation
2. Plan the emotional rhythm of the semester
   - plan for low intensity class sessions, e.g., a trip (on or off campus), showing a film, guest speaker, art activity, playing a game
   - plan for time during the semester for rest and reflection
3. Participate in peer support groups or professional support sessions
   - routinely talk with colleagues or friends throughout the semester

- contract a therapist, spiritual director, cleric, or counsel

4. Be aware of burnout symptoms

   - know (and monitor) the symptoms of depression, burnout, fatigue
   - journal concerning your emotional health as pertains to teaching

5. Be mindful of your own humanness

   - make sure you do not teach while over-tired or sleep deprived
   - be well hydrated and not hungry in the classroom
   - dress in clothes that make you feel confident and that are comfortable

We must find ways to stay emotionally connected while attending to our own needs. The emotional strain of teaching is part of the job but does not have to be a detriment of the job.

FOR REFLECTION . . .

1. What are the moments that renew you in teaching? How can you plan for those moments?
2. How do you plan your sessions so there is a rhythm to the semester?
3. What conversations or practices help you stay grounded?
4. What habits, practices, and behaviors help you sustain your truest self in the classroom?
5. What toolkit can you build for your emotional health and wellbeing?

11

Permission Giving

THE WABASH CENTER TEACHES toward freedom in hopes of liberation and healing. We have learned that acts of freedom occur in many forms and occasionally involve receiving permission. Since 2019, I have had the honor of reading the feedback forms completed by participants at the end of events and programming experiences. In addition to reading the feedback, there are regular occasions of extemporaneous comments from participants about the insights they have gained during the convened conversations. There is a reoccurring theme: the experience of having been given permission. Colleagues have reported having received permission to move toward new habits, practices, attitudes, approaches, and aspirations. Permission to strive for improved teaching is a key theme. Permission to expect more care, consideration, and regard from the institutions by which our participants are employed is often mentioned.

Much of this feedback comes from early-career colleagues for whom learning to navigate faculty culture is new. Similarly, there are a significant number of seasoned colleagues for whom the Wabash Center–sponsored conversations are life-giving and permission providing.

I hear gratitude in this feedback. More importantly, I hear that the giving of permission has been moments of empowerment, agency, healing, and inspiration toward freedom. I want to share with you a list of the kinds of permissions that are reported in hopes that you too might be encouraged toward new freedoms.

Participants have said, "I received permission to . . ."

1. develop my own voice, to speak up and speak out without embarrassment, fear, or guilt;
2. take the authority given me by my role and responsibility through hire, tenure, or promotion;
3. think differently about the established traditions or about the outmoded presumptions of my institution or academic field;
4. rather than give my power away, make decisions that are faithful to my values and ethics;
5. command and adjust my own syllabus in my own courses;
6. act as a good citizen in my institution in ways that align with my own needs, wants, aspirations, desires, and longing; to work in integrity;
7. prioritize my mental or physical health and the wellbeing of my family;
8. teach across disciplines for the benefit of my students and in ways that meet their expressed curiosities;
9. strive for a work/life balance and maintain that balance over my career;
10. say "No" to requests that do not suit me or that would overload or overwhelm me;
11. ask that I be called by the name of my choosing (with or without title) and that my name be correctly pronounced;
12. report acts of bullying and aggression against me or others;
13. seek counseling, coaching, mentoring, spiritual direction throughout my career;
14. take the time and needed psychic space to grieve over the failure of a significant achievement or the loss of a beloved;
15. be creative and imaginative and to wonder as an approach to teaching;
16. pursue outside interests, hobbies, and play;
17. resist grind culture, to resist productivity at the expense of my own wellness or the wellness of my family;
18. communicate when acts of violence like racism, sexism, classism, homophobia occur;

19. parse between the obligations of my scholar/teacher identity and my employment duties; and
20. rest.

The list is in no way comprehensive or exhaustive. I give you the list so you can see the kinds of issues that need to be attended to so that a healthy work environment is created and maintained. It takes hard work to move from a toxic and unhealthy culture to a culture of care, belonging, and justice. Perhaps giving permission to individuals to make healthy communal choices is a start.

FOR REFLECTION . . .

1. From the list, what permissions would benefit you and why?
2. Create a ritual for giving yourself permission. Recite, each morning for one month, two to three sentences that give yourself permission for what is needed to be healthier and more satisfied.
3. Add to the above list any permissions for which you need to improve your teaching or teaching life. Consider having a conversation with your department head or dean on ways to institute these permissions.

12

Take a Load Off

THE FOUR-DAY MEETING WAS held in a mid-town Atlanta hotel. The final session was filled with cheerful goodbyes and promises of continued conversation. After lunch the participants left for the airport. Wabash Center staff members Rachel Mills, Paul Utterback, and I were going home the next day. About 2 p.m. the three of us sat together in one of the first-floor lounges of the hotel. We were debriefing and making plans for the next event. Without warning the electricity went out. The hotel's backup generators did not turn on. The sudden darkness of the building, even with afternoon sunlight streaming into the large lobby windows, brought an uneasy feeling. Hotel staff rushed to rescue people trapped in the elevators. Arriving guests were unable to check into rooms. Guests who had been in rooms walked down the stairs and found seats in the lobby and lounges. We, along with the many other guests, were instructed to wait in the hotel bar. We were offered free cocktails and promised that the electricity would soon be restored.

By 6 p.m., still without power, we went to a nearby restaurant for dinner. The restaurant and all the shops in the area had electricity. After lingering for a very long time in the Indian restaurant, we returned to the hotel feeling confident that given the amount of time that had passed the hotel's electricity surely would be restored.

We entered the hotel lobby through the circular doors, and it felt as if we had gone through a portal into a disaster zone. Without the sunlight streaming through the large glass windows, the hotel lobby was mostly dark. The power loss meant little ventilation. The air was stale and uncomfortable.

Flickers of light from cell phones and laptops were sprinkled around the large room. People were sitting on the furniture surrounded by their luggage. People were propped up on the floor along the walls. Everyone looked forlorn. There was a dank self-pity, heavy in the air. I heard a mother trying to comfort a crying infant. No staff person was at the registration desk. Muffled conversations on cell phones and whispered talking in small groups increased the eerie circumstance. A few people sat alone, staring off into space, looking drowsy and angry. The usually active pool table and ping pong table were unoccupied. One man had fallen asleep on the couch and was loudly snoring.

We made our way through the crowd and back to the bar area where we had spent several hours in the afternoon. The mood at the bar was equally gloomy. The bartender noticed us and waved us over to where he was standing. As if he was passing along a secret, the bartender informed us that power had been restored on floors 6, 7, and 8. He asked us where our rooms were. Our rooms were on the sixth floor. The bartender said, "Follow me." We obeyed. The bartender guided us through the crowd to a side door of the hotel and out into a small alley. He told us to get in line. We joined a line of people who were going to walk up an outside fire escape to the floors with power.

As we started marching up the unlit stairwell, I was nervous. I was unsure if my arthritic knees could climb the six flights. I walked behind Rachel, who was behind Paul. There were many people climbing in front of Paul but only a few people behind me. Hotel staff had placed plastic glow sticks on the stairs and at the landings. The dimly lit staircase was creepy. The moment felt unsafe, even dangerous.

As we ascended, the climbing pace was slow, but steady. The woman in front of Paul dragged her luggage. Her suitcase hit every step, making a sound that was loud and unsettling. After two flights of stairs, the woman's breathing became labored. The sound of her bag hitting every step and her heavy breathing amplified the precarity of our situation. Still climbing, I heard Paul say to the woman ahead of him, "Ma'am, can I carry your luggage?" Through her wheeze and shallow breathing, the woman responded to Paul, "No."

After another slow-paced flight of stairs, and over the thump, thump, thump sound of the dragging luggage, Paul asked again, "Ma'am, I don't mind. Can I help you with your luggage?" She did not answer immediately, but when she answered she said, "No." I wanted to scream out and tell the woman, "Let him help you with your luggage, damn it!" But I did not. I was afraid that an emphatic interjection from me would make an already bad situation worse. By the time we got to the fifth floor, with her breathing quite loud, Paul asked the woman ahead of him again. He was almost pleading, "I can carry your luggage. I don't mind." The woman, a third time, said, "No."

When Paul, Rachel, and I got to the sixth-floor landing, a hotel staff person with a glow stick in his hand was holding open the hallway door. We walked past the man and into the lit corridor. As I crossed the threshold, I said a prayer, "Thank you." The doorman mistook my prayer as gratitude to him and he replied, "You're welcome." I was grateful to all who had given us safe passage up the dark staircase. We walked to our rooms, spent a restless night in the hotel, then checked out early the next morning.

I suspect the woman walking ahead of Paul got to her room.

I do not know.

I hope she did not need medical attention later that night.

Now, months after this harrowing event, I am haunted. I am haunted by the sound of the woman's labored breathing, as well as by the sound of her luggage hitting every step of the six flights of stairs. My haunting has lingering questions.

QUESTION ONE

Why was the woman unable or unwilling to accept help in her moment of distress and anxiety? We are accustomed to experiences of needing help with no help being offered; or needing help but no help being available; or needing help but help is not possible or too expensive or reserved for someone else. But this situation was none of that. Paul offered and was quite able to carry the woman's luggage. He noticed her dilemma and offered to help. Why was his offer of assistance refused?

We can speculate on the reasons Paul's gesture of help might have been declined. Perhaps the woman was too afraid to trust Paul and believed if he carried her luggage then she would owe him a debt or she would owe him a favor in return? Maybe she despised chivalry and refused the genteel gestures of all men? Or, perhaps she was used to doing everything for herself. Maybe she genuinely did not think that—through her wheezing and dragging of luggage—she needed help.

QUESTION TWO

Why, for the good of the others climbing the stairwell, did the woman refuse the offer of help? Surely, she could hear the loud, exasperating sound made by dragging her luggage and how this was nerve wracking for others. Surely, she felt the ways that that sound exacerbated an already bad situation. Why, in considering the needs of the group, did she not know that relieving her burden would lower the collective anxiety? Did she know and not care?

In the woman's defense, maybe it is easier to accept help when we are not traveling alone. Maybe accepting help requires that we are not riddled with fear or struggling to breathe. Or, maybe it is easier to accept help from people we know and trust. Maybe she had previously been betrayed by strangers offering assistance in the dark.

Is it better to only rely upon yourself?

Accepting help can demonstrate that you, like all of us, have limitations, weaknesses, inadequacies, and needs. Receiving help shows that there are others who have more capacity, more ability, are better fit, or are more prepared. The vulnerability of showing our needs might be too much for our egos or for our self-understandings. Perhaps we like thinking of ourselves as self-contained, self-reliant, and in no way dependent. What do our refusals of help cost the community? What is at stake for the community when individuals refuse assistance?

Living with the illusion of independence in the teaching life can result in long, uphill journeys of dragging too much stuff and straining to breathe. What would it take for our teaching journeys not to be onerous, especially when help is offered? What if agreeing to accept help becomes part of the culture of our faculties?

So that we might learn from this peculiar situation in ways that might strengthen our teaching and teaching life, ask yourself:

- When have I been the woman dragging my bag up hundreds of stairs, while gasping for breath, and refusing assistance when offered?
- When has my judgment about my teaching and teaching life been so poor as to refuse help?
- When could my burden have been relieved had I said yes to an offer of assistance?
- When was I unable to see that help for me would have benefited the community?

- When is it necessary to refuse help and when is it foolish?

FOR REFLECTION . . .

1. Identify a burden in your teaching or teaching life. Ask for help.
2. Identify ways you carry too much baggage. Ask for help.
3. Identify colleagues who are struggling in their teaching or teaching life and offer help.

PART TWO

Students—Coming to Know Adult Learners

Who are these adult students? How do I connect with their worlds and honor their realities? In what ways do we influence each other? What are my hopes for them? What do I do with the pain I feel and see in others? How do I prepare them?

13

Harness the Power at Your Disposal

TEACHERS OF RELIGION AND THEOLOGY recognize, from preparation and experience, the complexity of teaching fields of study in which students have a personal stake. Students, whether enrolled in courses on religion or theology, often base their engagement in the course with their personal faith, their personal moral codes, their personal ethics, decisions, and behaviors. Even if the course is not intended for this purpose, students signal with their questions and participation that they are thinking of the course materials through the lens of their own lives. Teachers cannot escape inquiries about events in the news that shake us daily and affect lives. Learning is always personal.

Our classrooms are permeated with questions, concerns, and issues that arise out of that which grips the attention of our nation and the world. In all moments, we are gripped by wars, social violences, global upheaval, and unrest. And we are aware that a society grappling with political, economic, and civic issues is also then challenged by people suffering with depression, insomnia, increased suicide, grief/loss, effects of domestic violence, increased drug addiction and abuse, exile into the prison industrial complex—to name a few. On any given day, and in any given class session, these issues are at play. Not anticipating conversations around these topics, ignoring the potential for these conversations, and/or declaring that these conversations are "inappropriate" will only serve to further the suspicion that the scholarly discourses of theology and religion are irrelevant, outmoded, and unnecessary.

Our students, in their insistence and persistence, declare to us that we have arrived at an inflection point in world history. What we teach and how we teach at this moment is critical to our survival. The stakes are high for teaching because its practice is one of the most powerful apparatuses of change in any society. What will it mean to harness this power? What will be lost if we do not? For those of us charged with teaching in this moment it is easy to lose sight, given all that is swirling, of our purpose. The aim of educational leadership in this right-now moment is to imagine, design, and build new routes into beauty, health, compassion, citizenry, community, and imagination. We must recognize that this moment of chaos and upheaval is also a moment of opportunity. In this moment of seeming impossibility, leaders/teachers must muster the wherewithal to envision a future that is whole, healthy, and just, for all. And then we must build that future, together.

The good news is that we are scholars trained in critical thinking and analysis. We know how to interrogate for the solving of complex problems. Large scale and huge scope problems are our jam! We are faculties of people capable of thinking toward new visions, dreaming new dreams, and we can learn to relinquish that which no longer sustains us. We know how to disrupt narratives of systemic hatred, systems of injustice, and tear down conditions under which people live one form of debilitating violence or another. Our advocacy matters. The difficult news is that we are unsure if we want to insist upon institutional nimbleness, adaptation, creativity, and empathy. If and how we are nimble as we react to the complex challenges of positive and negative changes will determine our survival. Our ability to adapt to new realities will be key to opening our future. The ways in which we care for ourselves and others will make a difference in our endurance. We have what we need; and we must not hesitate to empower those who are courageous, those who know how to design for a new future. Our classrooms are just the places for this work.

So, we ask for people, colleagues, in and beyond the academy, to reveal themselves for our benefit and learning: Who knows the skills, habits, and practices of redesigning? Who can assist us reconceiving our schools? Who are our best strategists? Who has the know-how for institutional creativity, imagination, and rebuilding? Who can draw blueprints for the new and the needed? Who understands nimbleness and can train us? Who adapts well and quickly and can teach us? Who sees that there are multiple realities and can show us? Who can lead us into our hopeful future? Our students have interests, skills, and abilities to assist.

Friends, we must, in dramatic ways, pivot the current educational enterprise that would have us stand by silently, passively, and complicitly to a world that would kill needlessly. We need leadership who will cause us to come together, be together, stay together to do whatever we can, to do whatever it takes, as teachers and scholars, to save our shared future. Do not go numb. Do not stop breathing. Do not avert your eyes, lower your head, or go invisible. Do not get used to the death toll reports. Be disturbed. Dare to hope. Be about teaching that is relevant and timely and attends to the needs of those yearning to live. The power of teaching is at your disposal. Harness it!

FOR REFLECTION . . .

Think about the students in a recent class you have taught, or think about a class you are teaching now.

1. Make a list of the students who have raised questions that point to personal involvement, push boundaries, challenge the status quo, and suggest the need for significant change. Make note of their questions concerning morality, personal vocation, character, and faith.
2. What would it take to organize their energies and inquiries for an all-school lecture, art exhibit, or field trip?

14

Diversity Complicates Our Seeing

Author's Note: My use of the word "diversity" is with reluctance. It is an overused and often misunderstood word. In this case, by diversity I mean difference. I am concerned with the difference that is revealed in our body sizes, shapes, shades, smells, tastes, and sounds. Diversity exists between cultures when minoritized peoples are compared to the status quo, or when white, Western, male, straight culture is normalized as superior. By diversity I mean to imply the innovation that is needed to meet the needs of classrooms when curriculum, rather than ignoring minoritized students, shifts to include, accommodate, incorporate, and value new meaning-making, new knowledges, and new ways of being together. Where there is diversity, there is likely conflict. Diversity, whether by institutional intent or by happenstance, complicates our ability to see students.

Peekaboo! I see you!

Infants and parents all over the world play some version of this game. In view of the infant, the adult hides their face, pops back into view of the infant, then says Peekaboo! . . . I see you! This game, full of surprise and expectation, results in the infant's squeals of delight and amazement. For infants and parents, being seen is joyful. Like in the peekaboo game, teachers understand the value and joy of conveying to our students that "I see you." It is important that each student in our classrooms have the experience of being acknowledged and welcome. Each soul wants to be seen.

With comparatively little effort on the teacher's part, students with similar aspirations, similar race, similar culture, and similar economic class easily find their place in the classroom tableau. It is less complicated to teach a course whose student population is homogenous than it is to teach in diversity. In sameness, the assumptions, the presumptions, the conventions, the ascribed values, and the norms function without need for explanation or clarity and typically without threat of contestation. "Everybody knows . . ." is the working premise—and rightfully so.

In the diverse classroom, "everybody knows . . ." falls short because now every body is not the presumed same body. In diversity, the bodies vary, the knowledges and know-hows vary. Differing bodies bring different music, clothing, hairstyles, lifestyles, languages, value patterns, religions, foods, history, health, and family situations. That which could be presumed as being normative can no longer be presumed and often demands a stretching of our thinking, being, understanding, and doing.

Our language, social labeling, and identity politics bear out our societal patterns of inclusion and exclusion. "In this country American is white. Everybody else has to hyphenate," said Toni Morrison.[1] When our white classrooms shift to include hyphenated persons, we are unprepared. Those students who, with their very presence, create diversity are often the students who go unseen and who are rendered un-seeable.

Regrettably and commonly, seeing minoritized students means policing them. The surveilling gaze, the suspicious stare, the apprehensive look, or the disapproving glance lets him/her/they know of the hostility and the relegation to being as a stranger. Or worse yet, students who create diversity in the school's population are erased, made invisible, removed completely from the sighted reality of the teacher. These students are ghosted—absented in classrooms. Their differences are not recognizable as adequate. Differences do not mean deficiencies.

As teachers, we choose which students we will see and which students we will disregard, look past, or look away from. This is a challenging realization. It is disingenuous for any teacher to say that he/she/they pays attention to all students, that they are able to see all students, that they are attentive to all students. Even the most caring teacher has students to which giving their attention is a strain. We all have biases, prejudices, and cultural insensitivities. This does not make any teacher a bad teacher. It does make us human beings who must learn to stretch beyond our prejudices, shallow cultural boundaries, and narrow sensibilities.

1. Morrison, "Interview."

Homo sapiens. "(Wo)Man who knows." Or rather, "human who is conscious." Human who is conscious that he/she/they does not know. We are our most human when we make choices, when we exercise the power of choice. Teaching is a testing ground, and learning place, for our own humanity. In teaching relationships, we succeed, or we fail miserably, by choosing to see some students and refusing to see others. It is this choice that makes us human and this choice that makes us good, bad, or growing teachers. In our humanness we are both vulnerable and afraid. The challenge is to muster the courage to see all the students—those like us and those so different from us that we shrink back and recoil.

FOR REFLECTION . . .

1. What does it mean to teach in such a way that the erased student rematerializes?
2. What does it mean to teach in such a way that the invisible-ed student reappears?
3. What does it mean to teach in such a way that the unseen or overlooked student comes into focus?
4. What does it mean to teach in such a way that the hiding or hidden student peeks out from behind their wall?
5. What does it mean to teach in such a way that the voiceless student comes to voice?
6. Can we teach in such a way that the learning experience for all would not make sense or would have no meaning if there was an erased student in the conversation?
7. What would it mean to teach with such precision that lessons, to be successful, need the input, participation, knowledges, voice, and creativity of all the students?
8. What kind of teaching relates to the diversity of students in the classroom without asking that every student normalize or centralize the white, male, straight, wealthy culture?
9. What if teaching in diversity is too difficult, too demanding—creates too many problems? Then what?

15

Seeing the Possibility in Students

ONE DAY MY FATHER asked my brother and me why we had stopped roller-skating. In those days, roller skates were constructed out of skin-bruising, abrasive metal. The design of the skates required a metal key. By turning the metal key, the skate adjusted by lengthening or widening to fit to the child's sneakers. Once the adjusted metal clamps were tightened on the shoe, the leather strap was buckled around the ankle. Even with the key and the straps, never was the fit precise. Notoriously and painfully, the metal skates would fly off your foot in mid-skate thus hurling the skater into walls, into trees, into parked cars. Or, the ill-fitting skate simply tripped up the skater and you landed on the concrete sidewalk—sometimes face first. Skating was more dangerous than it was fun. We told Dad we stopped skating because the skates did not work well. We told him that they kept falling off. We told him we were tired of getting hurt. With this conversation, my brother and I were hoping for new skates—the kind that were all-in-one with the attached shoe. These better skates had a rubber attachment on the toe to help the skater slow down. I wanted white skates and my brother wanted black skates. My dad saw other possibilities.

I do not remember if it was hours, days, or weeks after the initial conversation about the under-used skates that my dad redesigned our toys. The next time Brent and I saw our skates, Dad had turned them into scooters. Dad dismantled the skates and used found items from our basement and his own ingenuity. Dad made three scooters. One scooter had a metal milk crate as its console, was low to the ground, and was meant to be ridden on one knee. The other two were ridden while standing up—one with a wooden handlebar to grip while attempting jumps or fishtailing. The third scooter was more like a modified skateboard that required excellent balance. All the scooters had metal wheels—no key or leather strap was needed. My brother and I, plus all the kids in our neighborhood, played with those scooters for years and years. As I look back, my dad's nurturing of the possible was quite remarkable.

My dad had a thing about wheels for children. Dad believed children should be able to go! They should be able to travel, to have adventures, to explore—to see what there was to see. For him, wheels were a way for children to experience the world with imagination and possibility. Dad thought children should be in motion; he thought a child's impulse to go! should be kindled. The rule in our house was that once your feet could reach the brake and gas pedals and you could see over the steering wheel—you could drive the car. My brother and I started driving when we were ages ten and eleven, respectively.

Dad's ethic of go! did not stop with his parenting but was part of his vocational sensibilities. Dad was a school psychologist, special education teacher, and reading specialist. He was, for more than thirty years, employed by the Philadelphia Public Schools. At his retirement party, I heard his coworkers tell story after story of the ways my father rescued children from incorrect placements in remedial education classes. Countless times, when other psychologists would deem that a child had no possibility to learn, to read, to excel—Dad saw possibility in the child. My father retested children who other colleagues had previously tested. Often, his report would be that the children had a higher IQ and fewer learning obstacles than previously diagnosed. My father was regularly called as an expert witness in Family Court to dispute the misdiagnosis and misplacement of children in private educational systems. My father was an advocate for children because he could see them. Dad was known by his colleagues to be able to see the possibility in even the most dulled child.

I am not saying that my dad was optimistic or hopeful or even cheerful. Most days he was none of these things. What Dad modeled for our family and gave to the children he worked for in the public schools was much more substantive. My dad was imaginative. He would see possibility—in skates and in children. He could see children labeled as "retarded" or "learning disabled" as being productive, normal, healthy, contributing members of our community with value, worth, and dignity.

An unwritten responsibility of teaching is to see the possibility in students that they cannot see in themselves. Seeing the possibility in students is not a mystical gift reserved for only a few intuitive teachers. Seeing the possibility in students is about thinking up options, designing opportunities, engineering alternatives, redesigning what is offered, resisting rules that would stymie and oppress, and instead, set people in motion. Teaching is about providing wheels and the permission to go! Seeing the possibility in students is about looking at the student, then looking beyond the student knowing the wheels you provide are taking them into their future, and it is into that future that they must go.

FOR REFLECTION . . .

1. What would it mean to include in your syllabus multiple ways to earn a high grade? What would it take to adjust your assignments for students who are not strong readers or strong writers?
2. When your school's admissions committee convenes, do they consider more than GPA for admission? If so, what factors are considered? If not, what factors might be considered to have a wider variety of students with a wider variety of learning abilities? How does the faculty prepare for this wider variety of learning?
3. What learning activities or assignments can you design to help students move beyond learning "one way" and toward developing the capacity to see possibility as a learning outcome?

16

Applaud Wildly

THE POWER OF AFFIRMATION lies in the acknowledgment of a job well done. When colleagues applaud our success, we feel more a part of the enterprise, more connected, and more accepted. Being affirmed is being seen, noticed, made visible in erasing workplaces where so much of our work feels like it goes unnoticed or is simply taken for granted. Feelings of isolation and separation are lightened with applause.

Recently, I facilitated a workshop on teamwork and collaboration for a group of women who work as administrative assistants for a large corporation. For the most part, they feel unappreciated and undervalued. I led them in an activity that was intended to spark appreciation among them. I divided them into pairs and instructed each pair to interview the other. The interviewee was to share two of her recent successes at work. Then the roles were switched. When it came time to report back, each pair member was told to tell the entire group one of the interviewee's successes for which the entire group would then applaud wildly. I gave the instructions and asked if there were any questions. One woman commented that if we applaud too loudly security might come. I told her we would risk it. The group quickly divided into pairs and began the conversations.

After a bit, I reconvened the group and asked the first pair to report. I reminded the group to get ready to applaud each person. The first woman told of her partner's success. I began applauding and the group members joined in. With each success story, I extended the applause and added a cheer and called out the woman's name. The group followed suit. Smiles appeared on each face, and the woman being applauded sat up a little straighter in her chair and smiled—a little bit. By the time we finished, the energy in the room was vibrant. It was an affirmation fest!

At the end of the last session, as our benediction, we repeated the exercise. Rather than being interviewed, each woman told of an accomplishment she had in the last week or so. Without prompting, the women applauded wildly for each other. Security did not come. I encouraged the women to find ways to routinely inquire about each other's professional successes as well as personal accomplishments. I ended the session, gathered my belongings, and opened the door to leave. A senior executive was standing in the hallway. He looked surprised when the door opened. He commented, without smiling or making eye contact, in a chastising tone, "You all are very raucous." I said, "We most certainly are," as I walked past him without stopping.

The postal service was still the preferred mode of communication for important documents when I was working on my dissertation. I had sent my advisor a draft of two chapters. When the mail was delivered to our home, there was a thick, thick envelope. I looked at the address label. The huge envelope was for me, from my advisor. My heart sank. I was mortified. Why was the package sooo thick? I assumed that she did not like my work and included the paperwork needed for me to withdraw from the program. I assumed she hated my work and wrote, in many pages, to inform me of my inadequacy. My fears paralyzed me. I left the package unopened for a day—too afraid to open it.

Finally—after having driven my family crazy with my whining and self-criticism—I opened the package. Much to my surprise, relief, and delight, my advisor had so thoroughly read my work that her comments, affirmations, and edits were two pages for every one page I had written. My advisor had done the closest read I had ever received on my work. Her extensive comments were on the ways I could continue to strengthen already sound chapters. Her affirmation reduced me to tears. What she thought of my work meant the world to me. Hearing that my work was good and could be made better was a life-changing experience. Knowing that she pored over my work, considered my assertions, and resonated with my argument made me take my own thoughts more seriously. It made me want to write better, deeper, more clearly. She had sent me a package of affirmation.

When I was in elementary school, on report card day, my brother and I received one dollar for every A, fifty cents for every B, nothing for a C, and we owed our parents for anything lower than a C. My parents were not paying us for the grades we made. They were affirming us, in a very tangible and pleasant way, for our hard work. They were teaching us that our good grades needed to be celebrated. They wanted us to know that our good grades were noticed and that our good grades were a point of pride. After we were paid by my father, my brother would ask to go to the store so he could spend his bounty. I, more frugal, put mine in the log cabin bank on my dresser. I was planning on buying a blue Ford Mustang on my sixteenth birthday.

When I was on a faculty we had a ritual that was for me quite meaningful. At faculty meetings, when someone was tenured and promoted, we read aloud excerpts of the letter sent to the Trustee Board. The excerpts extolled the value of the work by the celebrated colleague. The excerpts referred to their successes and accomplishments and proclaimed the good efforts of the colleague. Once the words were spoken, the colleague received thunderous applause, and the entire faculty lifted champagne glasses and toasted the colleague for a job well done. It is an elegant gesture. It is a moment when the collected body affirmed the individual for the contribution made for the flourishing of the whole. It was a lovely moment that imbued respect, regard, and dignity.

Performance, per se, is not the world I know. Beyond third grade, I have never taken a bow with other cast members of a play; I have never bowed after performing with a band or choir. What I have experienced is, after giving a scholarly paper at a guild meeting, noticing the decibels of applause after my paper. In those moments, I am appreciative of the applause. If/when the applause seems to linger, even a bit, I am especially pleased that the audience signals their affirmation of my work. It is a small thing, but it sustains me, lifts me.

A challenge of teaching adult students is that they want to be affirmed for what they already know. When the desire for affirmation is at the expense of openness to learning, this is not applause worthy. Refusing to learn, yet still wanting applause, can be disconcerting to the hopeful teacher. I recently survived end-of-the-semester presentations. For the students who engaged the assignment, worked at exploring new materials, and created a meaningful and feasible project, I gave strong and clear affirmation. For at least three students I clapped loudly, uproariously, gladly. For the students who presented half-baked projects that lacked thoughtfulness and made me, at times, question my vocational choices, I did not give negative words of criticism. I instead sat in silence, withholding the anticipated affirmation.

Students seemed confused when their paltry presentations did not garner the expected "big" affirmation. I am disappointed when they choose to opt out of working hard in a course they have enrolled in under their own volition. I am amazed when they are confused about not getting affirmation for poor work.

Here's the thing about applause. It is a gracious and generous gesture that is needed by us all. It is not to be squandered or provided disingenuously. It is not to be demanded for lazy efforts. The sound of applause and the feeling it conjures is that for which so many of us yearn. This yearning is not selfish or grandiose. It is a heartfelt desire to do work that counts, to do work that is meaningful and held in high regard by our peers and elders. The applause of a single human being is of great consequence.

FOR REFLECTION . . .

1. Ask yourself—How do you applaud and praise students? How do you let them know when they shine? With mindfulness, praise your students more often.
2. We all question and challenge ourselves and our work. Too often we are lost in what we did not do, what we missed, or what we did poorly. Instead, think about one or two ways in the last two years you have seen learning, nurtured learning, fostered learning in your students. Applaud wildly for these accomplishments.
3. Collaborate on a faculty ritual that would applaud work well done. It might be just you with one other person. Or it might be the entire faculty learning to celebrate one another.

17

Keep Looking

THE NARRATION BELOW IS my recollection of a typical interchange between my mother and my father when I was a child. Be mindful that we lived in a large home, and invariably during these conversations my father would be on the first floor, and my mother would be on the second floor. So, as you read their exchange imagine loud voices between two people who cannot see one another.

> "Nancy, where is the wah-wah-wah!" said my father standing at the bottom of the staircase.
>
> My mother, likely sewing, or making beds, or doing some household work on the second floor, answered, "Look in the kitchen; in the drawer under the cabinet with the water glasses; it's on the left-hand side."
>
> Dad goes to the kitchen, opens a drawer, and rummages around the drawer, but cannot locate the wah-wah-wah. Dad returns to the bottom of the stairs to ask my mother again.
>
> "Nancy, I don't see it. It is not there."
>
> "Yes, it is! Look in the drawer—the one with the red handle; the wah-wah-wah is on the left-hand side," said my mother.

Dad returns to the kitchen. He checks to see if he had previously opened the correct drawer. He had not. This time he locates the drawer with the red handle, opens it, and rummages around in the drawer, but does not see the wah-wah-wah. A third time, he returns to the bottom of the stairs and in a louder, frustrated voice says,

"Nancy! It's not there. I can't find the wah-wah-wah!!!"

My mother, in a calm and loud voice, replies, "Keep looking!"

My father, convinced my mother is mistaken about the location of the wah-wah-wah, gives up. Acquainted with my father's sensibilities, my mother stops the work she is doing and goes downstairs to the kitchen. Hearing my mother's movements on the stairs (and our dogs running ahead of her as she walks), my father waits in the kitchen for my mother—glad she has come to find the wah-wah-wah for him. My mother walks past my father, pulls open the drawer under the cabinet with the water glasses, the drawer with the red handle. Seeing the jumbled contents of the drawer she makes a mental note to reorganize the drawer at dinner time. She reaches into the drawer, near the left-hand side, and pulls out the wah-wah-wah. Shocked, my father takes the wah-wah-wah and contritely kisses my mother on the cheek as thanks for finding it for him.

My question for reflection is not so much about my mother's skills of household item curation, but about my father's inability to see. Why could my father, even with the most specific directions, not see that for which he was searching? Or, why cannot our students, even with detailed syllabi, thick instructions for assignments, accomplish assignments? In other words, what does it take to see when searching?

One answer is perseverance. Keep looking!

My experience is that adult students want to Google once and call it research. Or they want to read once and expect to understand dense materials. Or they expect ChatGPT or other AI to produce a refined product with one command. When my mother instructed my father to "Keep looking!" she was calling for skills of perseverance. "Keep looking!" means that even if it is not in your experience or imagination (or the drawer you are rummaging through), it is in the imagination and knowledge of your teachers, so endure until you get to the end. As teachers, providing opportunities for our students to develop perseverance—the ability to keep looking until you can see it, find it, know it, understand it, get insight from it—is invaluable.

The inability for students to see is often vividly expressed in introductory classes. Teaching introductory courses often means that newly matriculated students' conveyance of what they know and the ways they approach the course is primarily through life experience or learnings from other degrees in other schools. New students grappling with new materials, new approaches, new vocabulary, and new praxis often make for frustrated learners and fearful adults. Adult learners, for the most part, do not like attempting the new. They prefer being affirmed for what they already know. For some, learning anew feels insulting, uncomfortable—as if it is personal judgment for not knowing what they should know. Studying religion and theology exacerbate these feelings of judgment—woulda' known, shoulda' known', and coulda' known are haunting experiences that free float in classrooms. For students who come from traditions steeped in particularly exacting ways of knowing sacred texts and sacred ways, the experience of not knowing can be devastating.

There were semesters I would assign one critical essay to be written over the duration of the entire semester. Incrementally, students would need to turn in drafts of the essay. Without assigning a grade, I would edit the draft, then return it for further research, thinking, and rewriting. At the end of the semester, the essay, now polished by the drafting process, would be submitted for grading. Many students let me know that this iterative process was emotionally very difficult. They did not want to keep "re-doing" the essay. They saw little value in moving from a weak version to a stronger version, especially if each version did not receive a grade. They found it challenging to keep looking for the same thing until it was found, created, written—well. This assignment exposed the narrow edges of their skills of perseverance.

At the risk of overworking an illustration, the previous scene of my parents' typical conversation has its limits concerning teaching and learning. Consider that my parents, as spouses of one another, did not have the contract of teacher and learner. A contract between student and teacher is a different contract than between husband and wife, parent and child, employer and employee. The contract between teacher and learner has its own distinctiveness. The contract between teacher and learner is meant to create space so the learner can disclose, be vulnerable, expose their curiosity and their want to expand and find insight. In return, the teacher provides opportunities for new knowledges and maturity. So, we must be mindful of the judgment call unique to the teacher/learner contract and the notion of perseverance.

In the moments before sight (understanding) by a learner, in the moments of frustration when what is searched for cannot be located or seen, the teacher has got to allow the learner the honor of the moment of not-knowing—the moment of struggle. For the teacher to rush in with the answer (rush in to rescue) is to deny the learner the moment of ah-ha! The ah-ha! moment of magic, achievement, and growth when what was searched for is found is why, in part, students want to learn. Teachers must be willing and able to stand in the moment when the student is frustrated and NOT act. In this moment it is easier to simply rescue them from the pain of learning, but resist. This is a truly difficult moment for teachers to hold. In these moments, we must learn to persevere.

FOR REFLECTION . . .

1. List one or two practices of teaching that you use regularly to assist students "to stand in the moment."
2. Learning takes time. New learning must interact with and engage old patterns. What is an assignment or practice you use to allow this interaction?
3. Step back and take a moment looking at your own teaching. What is a pattern or practice that is emerging that you want to nurture? Note specifically how you hope it will help students learn and connect with the passions at the heart of your class.

18

Knowing Better

Have you ever thought you knew something, only to discover, with the passing of time and the acquisition of experience, that there was more depth, breath, and nuance to the idea or situation than you had previously thought? Or, worse yet, have you ever found out that something you thought you knew was simply—inaccurate, outmoded, or outdated?

Physicists are still working to understand the nature of light as well as the nature of gravity. Every one hundred years or so there is a breakthrough that brings new clarity, more scientific accuracy, and a better grasp of the basic concepts of light and gravity. Each time there is a new discovery, fellow scientists work to refute, amend, and/or build upon the fresh claim. The intricacies of the universe are still being uncovered, discovered, and made known.

I want my students to approach their work like these physicists. I want them to work at contesting the current conventions of church/theology/faith as an obligation of religion. I want them, as part of their role and responsibility of religious leadership, to work toward new approaches, perspectives, and worldviews that will evidence the profound complexity of praising God and serving neighbor for such a time as this.

Alas, too often my students simply want me to tell them what to think—they say "Just tell us the truth / the recipe / the formula" . . . as if truth and theology are static, or even knowable.

I am trying to get my students to think new thoughts about old ideas. I am trying to get my students to think as if the context of the digital age has made us pioneers in a new social and religious experiment—because

I actually think it has. I want my students to yearn to know better. I want them to relentlessly pursue the new.

Reexamining what we thought we knew, nurturing curiosities for what others say is important, realizing that multiple, even opposing perspectives are likely simultaneously "right" while other tried-and-true perspectives need to be abandoned often leaves students flustered—especially those who came looking for the one true truth and the one true religion to match their own one call to ministry. Defending "one" in the age of multiplicity is like lashing yourself to the ship's mast in a high-tide thunderstorm.

I am aware that my students quickly learn rote answers to deep questions. They quickly read the culture and politics of the academy and substitute their "churchified" answers for answers provided by faculty. This is not increasing their knowing. This is simply trading the milk cow for the bag of magic beans.

Knowing better demands a suspicion that all there is to know has not yet been interrogated. It leans heavily upon the notion that God is mystery and God reveals God's self in God's own pace and rhythm. Students talk about God as if "he" is the uncle in the attic; as if all we need to know about God is known; as if the repertoire of God has been performed. Save us oh God from our lack of curiosity about you and your ways.

Knowing better is important to me, in part, because of my mentor Charles Foster. I am a womanist, an outspoken, unorthodox, sometimes Christian scholar shaped and influenced by a reserved, white man who passionately believes in the redemption of the world through the gospel of Jesus. People who do not understand the racial identity politics of the United States or of the racist/sexist academy are surprised to know my beloved mentor is a white man. My knowing better about speaking out against racism, sexism—the hegemonic forces of the US society—is possible, in part, because of the loving and steadfast nurturing I received from Chuck. A man of his convictions, he believed the New Testament writers who envisioned the Kin-dom of God as something other than a land of patriarchy and white supremacy. Even though he is not a womanist, Chuck gave birth to a womanist. The ways of God are remarkable—a holy mystery!

During a first session of Introduction to Educational Ministries, Chuck was on my mind. I thought of this quote. Charles Foster said, "The most serious threat to any community's future occurs when its education can no longer maintain its heritage into the present or renew its identity or vocation for its changing circumstances."[1] More than anything, I want my students to be able to maintain the changed and changing Christian heritage while finding new and needed ways to renew its identities and vocations all the while surviving in the unprecedented liminality of the twenty-first century. If we are to be Christian in the future, we need to pay attention to Chuck's wisdom in the present.

I want my students to be more than lukewarm church bureaucrats whose primary question of ministry is "Do the people like me?" Knowing better entails having an urgency about the relevance of a Christian vision for a pluralistic and technological global village—I learned this from Chuck.

FOR REFLECTION . . .

1. Think about the students in a class you are teaching. List two "new thoughts about old ideas," and "urgencies" you hope they acquire. Be mindful that when you teach the new you watch if your students consider the new or just gloss over it.
2. List the class practice or assignment that is allowing these questions to be asked and explored.
3. Now think about a mentor who shaped your teaching. Name the question/passion they called you to ask.

1. Foster, *Educating Congregations*, 23.

19

There's No Place Like Home

"Toto, we're not in Kansas anymore."

So many of our students have a "Dorothy" experience when they enter theological and religious education. Our classrooms are not that of which they have had previous experience. Our classrooms are not the local church, not Bible college, not the family reunion, not church camp, not church conference, not undergraduate school, not job site; not anything like they have ever had to traverse. The location of our adult classrooms, for many students, is unique. And, once the degree is received, it will be a space to which they never return. Our classrooms, for so many, are the most foreign space they have ever ventured into. So many students are out of their comfort zones. They are away from home.

While our teaching goals are rarely to comfort our students, teaching students who are upset, distressed, and skittish does not make for good teaching or good learning. Like many schools, we have a growing number of commuter students. The school where I was on faculty drew students from the boroughs of New York City, Jersey City, and Newark. While those of us who are familiar with living in the suburbs do not think of it as a "dangerous" space, those brothers and sisters who call the city home can find thick forests and dimly lit walking trails to be a problem.

One night after class I was walking home. Home was on the other side of campus. Between the building where I taught and my home was the baseball field, then an expanse of unlit trails through the campus arboretum. I had walked this route at night for many years with no fear or trepidation. After class, I passed a student getting into his car. Edgar (not his real name) was headed back to the city. We quickly exchanged after-class pleasantries, then I resumed my walk toward the woods. Edgar called out to me in a concerned tone, "Doc, where you headed?!" I turned around and told him I was headed home and said, "Good night." Edgar got in his car, raced around the parking lot until he caught up to me. He rolled down his car window and in a distressed tone called me to his car. I walked over—not sure what was wrong. He asked if I was going to walk through the woods—in the dark, alone. I said yes. He asked, "Please let me drive you home." Feeling Edgar's concern for me, I got in the car. During our five-minute drive, he expressed his anxiety for being in "the country." I told him I had lived here for many years and felt comfortable walking, even in the dark, in spaces I had come to know. He told me that if I needed a ride home after class for the rest of the semester that he would gladly drive me home.

Before this experience, I had considered that students might be uncomfortable with new ideas or new people or new values presented in our classrooms. I had not previously considered that students might be uncomfortable with being "in the country"—away from the city—uncomfortable in the terrain where they did not know the rules and the pathways were, literally, unlit. Suppose an obstacle to good teaching is the literal space we occupy? What if we have city people who have ventured to the country, or country people who have ventured to the city, and are fearful of this unfamiliar space? In either regard we have students who are distracted by their uncertain safety, worried if they will get back home safely and without incident. What does it mean to teach with this kind of discomfort in the room?

Dorothy, of *The Wizard of Oz*, turned her situation into a quest. She constructed a journey which eventuated in her return home. So many of our students are not on a quest; they simply want to get a degree and the degree-giving place is in a place that is very foreign, a long way from home, but commutable. They commute to the foreign place and then return home each week.

I suspect some students resign themselves to being uncomfortable for the duration of their education.

Complicating the discomfort and anxieties of our students, another dimension to their discomfort is the experience of possibility. Author bell hooks said, "The classroom remains the most radical space of possibility in the academy."[1] So many students resist encounters with "radical spaces of possibility" preferring instead spaces that are reliable and previously known.

My first teaching challenge was at age thirteen when I taught elementary-aged children in my church's summer day camp. Snack time was a favorite moment in the day's schedule. The teachers would gather all the children in one room and provide fruit as a snack. Ralph, age ten, never ate his fruit snack. He would complain and ask for cookies or chips. One day I sat with Ralph, who was pouting. I asked, in earnest, why he would not eat the fruit. He said, "Because you don't know what you're going to get." I told him that I did not understand.

Ralph said, "If you eat an orange, you don't know if it's gonna be sweet or sour. It might be juicy, or it might be nasty. But if you eat an Oreo—they all taste the same. You know what you're gonna get."

Many of our students find our classrooms too risky with possibility. They simply want to know, like Ralph, that they are going to get what they previously know, what they previously experienced as dependable. When we say learning will be discovery, newness, encounter with the unfamiliar, even transformative—the Ralphs in our classrooms recoil. They do not want to be transformed. Some of the resistance and anxiety is that lots of people do not have an adventuresome spirit. Or more to the point, students will say that in their busyness they do not have time for an adventure. The thought of new ideas is worrisome, even burdensome, rather than motivational or inspirational. Students' discomfort about risking the randomness of learning is anxiety producing and can make our classrooms woeful.

The spring semester is upon us, and my syllabus is prepared. Even so, I do not have strategies to relieve the many real discomforts, anxieties, and fears of my students. Edgars and Ralphs will likely be in my course as well as a few new kinds of fears I have yet to catalogue. By now I have enough experience to know that much learning can happen even when fears, uncertainties, and reservations are not calmed or eased. Beyond that, I know I need to be a nonanxious presence for the sake of all my students as well as for my own sake.

1. hooks, *Teaching to Transgress*, 12.

FOR REFLECTION . . .

1. Think about some of the realities of "home" students bring to your classes. Simply list several of them. How well do you know your students?
2. Look back over the list and note two or three that affect many of the students. Think about how you consider or do not consider these when planning class sessions.
3. What "possibilities" routinely challenge and frighten students? List four or five. As you examine the list, choose two. Think about how you invite these possibilities in your course design and syllabus.

20

I'll Get Fired

"Doc, if I teach what you are talking about, I'll get fired!"

"Talking about this in seminary is fine, but if I try to talk about white supremacy on my job—won't I get fired?"

"If I talk about racism and oppression in my church—I'll get fired."

In classroom conversations that teach against domination, systemic hatred, violence, and social dehumanization, students begin to consider what it might be like to take these agendas to the places where they have leadership responsibility, authority, and obligation. Students become concerned about what might be at stake should they take up the lofty ideals of equity, liberation, and social holiness. The concern for personal risk is not pervasive, but it is certainly a concern that is voiced. Once students learn a bit about employing liberative pedagogies they become concerned about employment stability, the consequences of moral agency, and the backlash of courageous acts. Students feel inspired, intrigued, and curious about new approaches to the sins of xenophobia, white nationalism, racism, misogyny, Islamophobia, and homophobia, only to be halted by the personal fear of communal rejection, the possibility of shunning, and the chance that they will get fired.

After reading great thinkers like bell hooks, Paulo Freire, Katie G. Cannon, Parker Palmer, and Audre Lorde, students lean into the conversation of social transformation and church accountability. They "try on" the ideas of liberation and the hope of systemic equity for minoritized people, economically disenfranchised people, and those seeking asylum. There is a thrill to these taboo and previously unconsidered notions of good community and spiritual maturity. Quickly though, too quickly, the thrill meanders into, or slams into, the reality of being a neophyte leader in an established system. Their questions wither into concerns of self-preservation and selfishness—"If I try to do this stuff, will I get fired?" Critical, prophetic wisdom shrivels. Rather than bringing ease, deep study plunges the student into discomfort, dilemma, and the promise of hardship, sacrifice, and possible loss of power, authority, and social stature.

In asking if they will get fired, I do not believe my students are having a crisis of conscience—their conscience is clear. They say they want liberation for all persons—and I believe them. Their dilemma is falling victim to the illusion of security. They are afraid that if they lead people toward change, and teach toward an ethic of compassion, love, empathy, and mercy, that this will be such a drastic shift away from the current norm of white supremacy and patriarchy that they will be punished. These genuine concerns must be considered in the seminary classroom if learning about justice is to be real and realized.

On the days I am impatient with their self-centered concerns, my answer to their genuine, albeit uninspired, concern is to quote science fiction writer Octavia Butler, "So be it. See to it."[1]

With this statement I am not so much trying to be callous as I am trying to portray what my Bible-reading grandmother told me: "We do not fight flesh and blood, but powers and principalities." What she meant was that we are obligated to speak our truth then trust in the Spirit who would see us through the fight; our truth and trust must be in God. This is a hard lesson that sometimes takes a lifetime. My grandmother would also import Emily Dickinson's advice to "tell the truth but tell it slant," her version of "be wise as serpents and innocent as doves" (Matt 10:16).

When I am more patient, I linger over the question of self-preservation. I carefully explain that the work of teaching to transgress, if done effectively, will likely result at some point in life with the loss of favor, friends, reputation, money, and yes, might result in getting fired. I want my students, even the young ones, to have more fear of the harm and violence of living in a racist society than fear of personal sacrifice. I want them to fear being unfaithful to what they say they care about and believe. I want their fear to motivate them rather than paralyze them.

1. Butler, *Parable of the Sower*, n.p.

When I ask the student who had the courage to voice their fear of being fired why they would want to lead a congregation or institution that would suppress their impulse to fight against the status quo, I am asking why they would want to squander the gifts they offer for the needs of the world to a people who are uninterested in, or unmoved by, the suffering of the world.

Heretofore, my students have heard this as a rhetorical inquiry, and no one has responded to this query—not yet.

I tell them that failure (like getting fired) is likely one of the better learning opportunities in the teaching journey. Surely, few of us have the wherewithal to prescribe failure or to sabotage our own career, even for justice work. However, when the surprise of failure finds us, we must know these likely signals of new opportunity, new fulfillment, the chance for deeper contemplation about the meanness of the world and our role of leadership. Some of my most creative teaching episodes have come from my failures. I must remember to tell my students more stories of when I failed, what I learned and, most important, point to the fact that I have lived to talk about it. Failure, even when deadly, has not yet meant my demise.

We tell students to live the question—or at least I do. But they must live the deeper questions and not the shallow ones. If their best reflection question is "Suppose I get fired?" then this narcissistic inquiry will embolden the status quo.

Shallow reflexive questions will only serve to undergird mediocrity and leave domination unchecked.

Living the big questions of life means, in the twenty-first century, coming to grips with the fact that there is no place to escape the diversity of the human community. Our pursuit of the deep questions from the public view of teaching will help other people to do things they really want to do but are too afraid to do by themselves. People want to be good neighbors, want to welcome the stranger, want to live in harmony with dignity, respect, and peace. Our job, as learned people, is to provide them with excuses, rationales, and ways to honor these virtues of justice. Those of us who are privileged to have studied cannot retreat into small, menial jobs of maintaining the status quo or regress into living quiet lives of desperation hoping to be rescued by the leadership of someone else. Those of us who are educated must take up the big, big, big jobs of life like teaching justice, spreading mercy, and modeling love. We must refuse to be seduced by shallow subsistence that promises a paycheck. Our job of justice is to enunciate so clearly that truth is unmistakable—the truth that there are no inferior people. This enunciation will likely get all of us fired.

FOR REFLECTION . . .

Remember a couple times when students have told you that they would be afraid to share an insight, course content, or new meaning in their work setting.

1. Think about if and how you challenge those fears.
2. Make a list of ways you seek in classes to assist students to address these fears.
3. Looking at yourself, note two or three commitments that empower your teaching. Name how you embody these in classes.
4. Thinking of a particular class, in what ways do you help students engage and claim a call for action?

21

Belong a Little Bit

Belonging is a yearning of the soul. Our life's quest is often about finding the place, purpose, or persons to which or to whom we belong. We need to feel at home; we yearn to feel accepted, swaddled by our relationships.

We want to experience being part of something bigger than our finite, individual, selves. The experience of belonging makes us keenly aware of the connectional joy of humanness. Equally, the experience of alienation, of having no place to call home, of being deemed inferior, is a profound experience of dehumanization and is soul dampening. Twenty-first-century racism would have minoritized people believe that we are "welcome," only then to be immersed in experiences of disrespect, disregard, and hatred. At best, this creates a psychic quandary for us. At worst, this harm is debilitating to our ability to teach and to learn. The magnitude of the need to belong necessitates a pedagogical priority, especially in those white schools with minoritized persons on faculty, on staff, and in the student body.

The seminary where I was on faculty is in an affluent New Jersey suburb. The town is a bedroom community for executives and corporate giants of Manhattan. Consequently, we enjoy clean streets, splendid restaurants, a preponderance of shopping, great theatre, and a world-class jazz club. Also, consequently, is the existence of a clear two-tier caste society: those who live here and those who come to work as cashiers, waitresses, nannies, elder care workers, gardeners, and secretaries. I, due to faculty housing, live in this town. Typically, the workers who come to town are African American and Latine. The residents are typically white. I am routinely treated by fellow residents, as well as by commuter workers, as if I do not belong here. I am African American living in this affluent county—an embodied oxymoron, at best. I pay taxes here, vote here, work here, but, from the gaze of the racist eyeball, I do not belong here . . . I've lived here for twenty years.

Recently, I was having breakfast at the local diner with our dean, Javier Viera. Dean Viera, born in Puerto Rico, is fluent in Spanish. When the waitress came to our table to take our order, she was, as she always is, pleasant and, in retrospect, sad. I did not notice her sadness until it morphed into a smile. What made her smile was when Javier greeted her in Spanish and ordered his breakfast in Spanish. When Dean Viera spoke to her in Spanish it both surprised and delighted her. Her face lit up like a Christmas tree. At his speaking, she went from an almost invisible presence to a woman of dignity. This drastic shift happened when she was spoken to in a language that signaled her belonging—or more accurately, her shift happened when she received the signal that she was not alone, not alien. The dean could have ordered in English. I did. Instead, in that moment he chose a language that invited the waitress to know a little bit of who his people are, what his allegiances are, and the kind of man he is. In this moment of belonging, he code-switched.

A few years ago, I drove into the school parking lot and whipped into a space designated for faculty. I literally parked in front of the sign that read "Reserved for Faculty." Distracted by my own thoughts, I got out of my car, opened the back door to get my briefcase and bags, then shut both car doors. Still distracted as I walked, I headed up the path to the seminary building, intending to go straight to class. Joe (not his name) was a facilities staff person whose job it was to place temporary signs around campus for upcoming events. Joe had worked at the school longer than I had, and by that time I had been there for more than ten years. Joe, seeing me park in faculty parking, stopped hammering a signpost near the space where I parked. He shouted over to me, "You can't park there." In Black woman fashion, I decided I did not want to be bothered, this day, with this kind of #$%@##. Without replying or acknowledging him in any way (ignoring is a Black woman survival strategy), I kept walking. Joe raised his volume and shouted in my direction, "That's for faculty. YOU can't park there." As I entered the building I looked over my shoulder to see that the sign-man had left his assigned task and walked over to my car and was inspecting the parking tag in my car window. I suspect Sign-man was surprised when my tag read "Faculty." Even when I "belong," Sign-man, on the lowest tier of the hierarchy, believes he can police me and tell me that I do not belong. WTH! $%##*!

Though my enthusiasm at the start of any fall semester wanes, my clarity of purpose sharpens. At the end of the orientation worship service, I position myself in the hallway. As the new students leave the chapel, I ferret out the new African American and African students, shake their hands, read their name tags aloud. I ask in which degree program they are enrolled and inquire about their fall course selection. While doing this, I keep an eye on the stairway. If it looks like a student who I have not spoken with is going down the stairs, I, in true old-Black-church-woman style, snap my fingers to get his/her attention, then wave them over to me. As I corral each student, I use Black church gestures and tones telling them, do not wait for trouble, then decide to come find me; come sit in my office soon and we will get acquainted. I tell them to email me, and we will have coffee or lunch—soon. I want them from their first day to know, at least a little bit, that they are not alone in this place. I tell them that the protocols and practices of respect, decency, and regard of Black church culture are, with their presence, operative and that I am a representative of our shared culture. I want them to know that this school has something of merit to offer them if they can just figure out how to extract the best and leave the rest. I want my gesture to signal to them my availability to help with this leg of their holy journey. I tell them, I, like the other old women of our church tradition, in any given moment, can reach in and down to my DD-located coin-purse for a piece of money, a freshly pressed handkerchief, a peppermint candy, or a straight edge.

For me, the importance of this gesture is like what our dean did for the waitress. Or, more importantly, an antidote for when, not if, the sign-man speaks to them on our campus. I am trying to communicate, amid all the hollow rhetoric of "welcome," that they belong in our school because our people have fought and won the right for us to be in this place. I code-switch. I code-switch in earshot of the public to signal to the African and African American students, at least a little bit, that their racial/cultural identity is part of this place and that their/our expressions of religion, faith, values, and community are here, at least a little bit.

It does not take Jim/Jane Crow–era signs reading "Whites Only" at the water fountains and bathrooms to make people of color feel unwelcomed. Strategies of hatred and alienation are maintained in the DNA of the institution as well as by the sign-posters on payroll. By now, I have been at my desk long enough to have a modicum of authority, some institutional voice, and can exercise some mother's-milk–given moxie. At this stage, I possess less fear of reprisal or sabotage and more orneriness. My orneriness is one of the gifts of having survived into crone-hood; it is a gift from the ancestors, a pay-off of having earned the distinction of full professorship and being near retirement. As a person who has earned influence and power in this profession, I feel it my obligation to use this cachet to tell Black students that they belong and then to work until it happens.

This year, after my practice of greeting all the students of the African diaspora, I made my way to the foyer for the buffet lunch. I was joined in the queue by a tenure-track faculty colleague who is Korean. A new student came up to my colleague and, in greeting each other, they spoke in Korean. After the brief exchange, my colleague introduced me to the student in English. I was glad my colleague also understands the necessity of code-switching to assist Korean students in feeling that they belong, at least a little bit. Later that week, the same colleague and I went to dinner. We chose a sushi restaurant. The maître d' greeted us at the restaurant entrance, then sat us at a table. He took my friend's drink order in Korean and mine in English. Once the man left the table side—I playfully feigned insult and asked my friend why the maître d' had not spoken to me in Korean. My friend tipped his head forward and, looking at me over his glasses, smiled. The truth telling of his culturally familiar gesture made me laugh out loud.

FOR REFLECTION . . .

1. How do you work to get to know the students in your classes? Explicitly list three or four practices you use to acquaint yourself with students.
2. Ask a colleague or two their practices for acquainting themselves with students and their concerns.
3. In what ways do you work to help students build communities of learning in class?
4. How do you work with small collaborative groups in class so they can complete an assignment?

22

Tears About Miseducation

SOMETIMES LEARNING IS ACCOMPANIED by tears, theirs and mine.

The concept of miseducation is so disquieting to some students that tears are shed in the classroom. Never have there been bold sobs or muffled cries of languished sorrow—nothing quite so dramatic. Rather, the tears have been quiet moments of upset-ness that makes the nose run, the hands tremble. For a few students, tears well up, then the body tenses and clinches to control the tears from spilling over onto their cheeks. On two or three occasions, when the tears have overflowed their fleshy banks, she quietly left the room (usually she is a Black woman) to return after splashing cold water on her face and taking deep breaths while alone in the neutral space of the restroom. When she comes back to class, I smile at her—nod my head to affirm her strength.

When the tears come, I bear witness to the insight, revelation, grace, and pain.

I used to wait and IF it happened, IF tears came, I would then pray. Now—now I know to pray before I introduce the concept of miseducation so WHEN the tears bubble up my prayers have summoned salve for the reopened wounds that hopefully will heal (some wounds never heal). Sometimes teaching is the reopening of wounds.

The tears are not easy to see; they must be felt. People try to hide them. Students are caught off guard when an idea has the audacity to move them to tears. I first noticed because I felt the energy in the room quickly shift. Students become uncharacteristically fidgety. Hands reach into purses for tissues, faint sounds of sniffling dapple the airwaves, and eyes that usually meet mine look away; feet turn sideways, signaling loss of grounded-ness and disorientation. A shrilled quietness creeps in; their breath shallows and they close their eyes, gently gasping for ease. Oh, miseducation can be onerous to sit with.

Other students notice the shift in energy too, notice the tears—seen and unseen, flowing and damned up. Some students, in response to the tears of others, disconnect from the moment wishing to flee the intensity, the reality that pushes in like a home invasion in the suburbs when people, lying into TV news cameras, say, "Nothing like that ever happens around here." Others sympathetically move closer to their friend—consoling with proximity of care. Still others genuinely do not notice—so unplugged from the learning experience that nothing penetrates and nothing excretes—distracted; they just dangle through the semester.

It is difficult to teach concepts of oppression and dehumanization when those who have borne the brunt of the lash are in the room. Paradoxically, it is my joy to teach concepts of oppression and dehumanization when those who have borne the brunt of the lash are in the room. And of course, ironically, those who wielded the bullwhip, nightstick, and hanging rope are also present.

The disturbing and healing quote that is the catalyst for the tears is this. Carter G. Woodson, author of *The Mis-Education of the Negro* (1933), wrote,

> If you control a [person's] thinking, you do not have to worry about [her] action. When you determine what a [person] shall think, you do not have to concern yourself about what [she] will do. If you make a [person] feel that [she] is inferior, you do not have to compel [her] to accept inferior status, for [she] will seek it for himself [herself]. If you make a [person] think that [she] is justly an outcast, you do not have to order [her] to the back door. [She] will go without being told; and if there is no back door, [her] very nature will demand one.[1]

Sometimes, if I am not mindful, their tears will swiftly turn to anger, fury, closed-fisted guile . . . Since I myself am just a hair-trigger away from rage, I empathize, I ache, I struggle to push past my own madness to maintain our collective agenda of peace, liberty, and repair of the soul.

1. Woodson, *Mis-Education of the Negro*, 84–85.

More than anything, I respect their tears. To be moved, in a classroom, giving over to vulnerability is the heart that is still alive, still yearning, still desiring freedom. I respect anyone who traverses the death-dealing path of US education and can still cry about injustice.

Their tears rekindle my hope. Their tears are indicators of their courage to reach out into the unknown and discover those ancestors who are reaching to them—able to comfort, console, and heal.

FOR REFLECTION . . .

1. Think about three or four moments when you saw tears in the classroom. List the moments and under each name reasons for the tears.
2. Now name how you addressed, comforted, supported, engaged the tears.
3. Sometimes tears reflect deep anger. Name ways you allow anger to be expressed. Also name ways you walk beside students or help them walk beside each other in both expressing and addressing the anger.
4. Think about the injustices that your students face. Note ways you offer a place to express and share pain in classes.
5. Note how your class offers places to engage the pain students bring and ways to engage those pains.

23

Taking It Personally

MY FATHER, LLOYD R. WESTFIELD, spent much of his career as a school psychologist with the Philadelphia public school system. He loved his job, and by many accounts, he was very good at his job. I have vivid memories of him, one summer, as an adjunct professor for Temple University, teaching a course on abnormal psychology. His unanticipated challenge was that with the introduction and exploration of each psychological malady, students "diagnosed" themselves as having each abnormality. Dad said it was like watching children try on high heeled shoes, sequined church hats, feathery boas, and bright red lipstick in their mother's closet, except—these garments were distortions, emotional problems and diseases. The stress and duress of teaching students who were primarily doing self-serving analysis was exhausting for my father. When asked to teach the course the following summer—he declined.

Something similar happens in the adult classroom when teaching about issues of white supremacy, systemic racism, domination, identity, and societal violence. Students try on the social maladies of injustice as if trying on personal garments. In turn, their classroom engagement is reduced to gazing into the mirror looking for personal fit and failure. If the metaphorical garment somehow fits—they are ashamed. If the metaphorical garment, from their own imaginary inquiry, is ill fitting—they absolve themselves from personal responsibility. This venture into taking it personally turns into irresponsible reflection that serves to block critical reflection and hampers a sophisticated consideration for the issues of justice. Teaching in the disciplines of religion, culture studies, race theory, and gender studies means that all my classes are rife for the personal try ons.

As a womanist, I am deeply committed to the construction of knowledge that comes from personal knowing, experience, and the everydayness of living. For me, this is the source of wisdom and hope. At the risk of contradicting my previous paragraphs, I am making a distinction between knowledge production and playing at therapy; between reflecting upon personal experience and getting upset about the ideas we are studying because you think the ideas we are studying are directed, or aimed, at you.

The obstacle to teaching, as I see it, is when the classroom is reduced to a place where students haphazardly "play" at their own personal responsibility, and in so doing, refuse to immerse into critically responsible reflection. Students, when taking ideas personally, use the personal as an excuse to be dismissive, judgmental, or just plain rude. Taking issues personally withers the exploration of the personal experience.

It is a challenge to differentiate between white people and the ideology of white supremacy. It is a challenge to differentiate between the ideas of domination (patriarchy, racism, sexism, homophobia, classism, misogynoir) and the lived choices of our brothers and sisters. It is difficult to convey to students that "(this) is not about you—personally" when, for so many, this is the first or one of the first conversations that provides information about the workings of systemic oppression.

I am not suggesting an emotional disconnection from study. On the contrary, I have vivid, visceral memories of moments when theory has liberated me—personally. As well, I can recall moments when theory has eviscerated me—personally. It is nearly impossible to remain objective in deep, meaningful study. What I have learned is not to give over to these super-charged emotional experiences, but instead sit with them and ask, "What am I to learn?" The challenge of this kind of pedagogy is to teach students to sit with their own discomfort, and rather than wallow in anger or pity or pain, dare to press through to the new meanings, new learnings—to the change. Inviting students to have new thoughts about old ideas is inherently uncomfortable, likely tremendously emotional, and, if done successfully, will cause transformation of mind, body, and spirit. Lingering with, being present to, students who are learning to sit with their own discomfort might be the most difficult aspect of teaching. Of course, I am speaking personally.

FOR REFLECTION . . .

1. In what ways and how might we sit with students as they work through their discomfort with certain ideas? What does it mean to linger with students as they struggle?
2. In what ways/how does a professor signal a student that, while there is no room for "taking it personally," there is ample room to reflect on the personal experience?
3. Is it possible that we need to routinely refer students for professional therapy as they engage these large ideas of existence?

PART THREE

Classes—Contexts for Learning

In what ways do classes help students thrive, be inspired, claim agency? When do courses help them focus on the search for meaning, purpose, and vocation? What empowers them to action? How do I build communities of learning?

24

Judged by Your Behavior

Talk Is Cheap

Teaching is a human-to-human encounter.

Classroom spaces are places of intimacy and influence.

Course planning typically focuses on the many ways the academic content shapes, forms, and informs students. In our planning, what we too often underestimate, and under-plan for, is the personal encounter in the classroom.

Students learn as much from the person who teaches the course as they do from the assigned readings, lectures, and rubrics. Often, they are paying as much attention to the teacher as a person as they are to the theories, concepts and approaches being presented. What if the most formational elements of our courses are the ways we, implicitly and explicitly, perform them?

If we take a moment to consider the ways students learn more from the behaviors and attitudes of the professor than they do from the topic, we will realize that our classes are permeated by our beliefs and commitments. Your classroom behavior makes vivid your personal values.

Are you aware that your personal values are baked into and operative in your courses? Are the values that undergird your teaching aligned with the institutional values? Are you aware that your personal values are seeable, viewable, known by your students? If so, which of your behaviors are inconsistent with your personal values, and which personal values do you wish to make most evident in your teaching?

A facilitator at a recent staff development session I attended said, "We judge ourselves based on our intentions; others judge us by our behaviors." This resonated with me. In other words, it is not what you say, but what you do that tells your students your ethics. If you talk the talk without walking the walk, then you have formed students with confusion, misalignment, and uncertainty. Words, platitudes, and good intentions are shallow without observable actions.

It is not enough to have the intent of compassion, hope, courage, dignity—if no one has the experience of these values in interactions with you or through the learning assignments you guide and offer. Colleagues will often say they value such attributes as:

- learner-centered teaching but then lecture during most sessions, placing themselves as "the expert" in the center of the course and relegating the students to the margins of the conversation;
- community and partnership but assign only individualized assignments to be graded;
- collaboration but offer no group activities as approaches to learning;
- creativity but ask that students simply regurgitate information;
- reliability but rarely return graded assignments in a timely manner;
- persistence but provide no mechanism to award the student who begins the semester with low grades ways to improve the final grade;
- responsibility but provide for no major decisions for students to make concerning their own learning in the course;
- care and compassion for others but limit the scope of the course conversation without including neighborhood projects, adventures, or pilgrimages; or
- diversity without including voices other than those deemed as typical, commonplace, and regular.

Designing learning environments and experiences that are congruent with and exemplify your personal values will enhance the learning of your students. Creating this kind of integrity will foster learning experiences that nurture trust and instill confidence in your students.

FOR REFLECTION . . .

Our behaviors tell a story about who we are, what we value, and what we are about. How we behave toward one another speaks volumes and teaches lessons likely to last a lifetime. Sculpting congruence in the classroom can be challenging, even for the most seasoned teacher. Consider these activities to strengthen your teaching:

1. Ask a colleague to audit your syllabus for the personal values it communicates. Have a dialogue with the colleague about what they see, sense, and suspect about your values. Discuss ways to align the values you want to be operative in the course with the design of the course.
2. Make a list of your personal values. Reflect—ask yourself why you choose these specific values to be exemplified in your teaching. Describe behaviors, practices, and habits that are consistent with these personal values. Then, design or redesign a course with the list, rationale, and behaviors in mind.
3. Ask a colleague to observe your teaching for three weeks, six weeks, or an entire semester. Ask that they watch for your traits, behaviors, habits that demonstrate the values, beliefs, and philosophies you demonstrate in your classroom.
4. At the beginning of the semester, tell your students the values you are pursuing in the course. Decide, with the students, the behaviors that should be promoted for these values.
5. Reflect—with a trusted colleague—those behaviors that are inconsistent with your personal values that you portray in the classroom. Decide which one or two behaviors you will work on in the coming semester for better alignment.

25

Courses Are Not Words

One of the many joys of reading poetry is the fluidity of meaning to which poems lend themselves. Poets like Mary Oliver, Sonja Sanchez, Lucille Clifton, Paul Laurence Dunbar, Alice Walker inspire us to think beyond the words on the page and into reimagining our own situation. Poetry assures us that words are more than words. Words are bread for the journey, fire for the cold, and ropes let down for rescue.

Teachers! Can we make this declaration with firm regard and assuredness about our courses, our teaching, our livelihood as faculty? What would it mean if, with the help of poets, and audacity from deep within us, we whispered one to another: Our courses are not simply clever words but fires, meals, ropes—keys to unlock doors to eternity.

Often, I wonder what a course is, or what it is for. I know the mundane of why courses are taught. The curricular obvious and the institutional mechanics are part of my understanding; I am not asking about the obvious or the mechanical. Instead, I wonder if courses matter. Are courses important, impactful, and when they are—what makes them so? What makes a course fire? Rescue? Or sustenance for the poor?

Mostly, when I was enrolled in courses, very few experiences had the gravitas of the comparison with Mary Oliver's provocative images. Like most folks with a terminal degree, I was enrolled as a student in formal course work for over twenty years—if I start counting from kindergarten. In most cases, the teacher did not do anything wrong, but neither did they do anything like bringing fire for my warmth or letting a rope down when I was in a pit. And, I have inhabited cold, dank pits.

It is too easy to recount experiences of flimsy teaching, but their commonness is crippling to our students. By the second week of a required course in college, my friends and I figured out that the lectures of the professor were excerpts from the primary text. During the weekly hour-long lectures, we sat quietly in class and highlighted the passages she read aloud from the re-typed pages she laid on the podium. Occasionally, the teacher would skip pages in the text causing us to, with a flurry, turn pages until we found the passages to which she had jumped. I always wondered if she noticed that we were not taking notes but highlighting the textbook, and if so, what did she think about this. At midterm and final, in preparation for the tests, my friends memorized the passages in the book. I, thinking that a waste of time, got a B in the course because I refused to "study." I was bored in the course.

We have all survived teaching that has been reduced to words, facts, and data. Mary Oliver bids us to take stock of the possibility that teaching could be, after all, life changing and life-giving. Given this opportunity, it would behoove us to set our intentions as if we are about course design with transformative power. The power to feed the hungry, locate the lost, and set the captives free.

I have been a student in several courses where I received healing, inspiration, and renewed agency to meet my vocation well prepared. Some courses shifted my core values and deepened my commitments. Some courses were exemplars of a call to action for the rest of my career.

In 1985, one such course was titled Ministry and Mission of the Church in the World Today. It was co-taught by Jack Seymour and Robert O'Gorman. I found the course interesting, and equally, I was fascinated to watch the two scholars/friends as they taught. I learned as much by watching them teach as I did by being taught by them. Three sessions before the end of the semester, I found myself sitting in the classroom quite frustrated. Near the end of that day's lecture, I raised by hand and, fumbling for words, asked a question about implications and application. As was the established practice, each professor took a turn responding to my question. Both responses said that questions of implication were not part of this course. My frustration deepened. I furrowed my brow, frowned my face, and spoke back—vehemently. I, in graduate student authorial voice, informed my teachers that our conversation had to include conversation on implication because without that, I said, "What was this course for?" The two men were surprised by my outburst but not deterred. They said they would discuss my request. At the next class session, Jack and Bob informed us that they had adjusted the course syllabus for the final weeks. The new design now included two sessions focused on implications and applications. At the announcement, the class cheered! I was amazed and changed by having had my curiosity taken seriously.

I am not suggesting that all courses should include questions of implication. I am suggesting that, if we are intentional, courses can become spaces for teachers and students who, together, learn to kindle passions, braid ropes to lower sojourners over sheer cliffs, something as necessary as cool water in drought.

FOR REFLECTION . . .

1. Think about one of your courses. When is a time that you changed the syllabus considering student needs, comments, and your own imagination? Tell a friend and dialogue about the outcome(s).
2. Thinking about the same course, note the ways you hope it empowers students. List three or four of the consequences you hope it has.
3. Create a list of ways you solicit student feedback during a course. Consider ways to let students know you take their feedback and curiosities seriously.

26

Personal Policies List

REGARDLESS OF HOW MANY times pedagogical guru Parker Palmer is asked, he refuses to comply. Dr. Palmer, in his writings, speeches, and workshops, resists reducing the mystical adventure of critically reflective teaching to "tips, tricks, and techniques." While I agree wholeheartedly, I also know that what interests, challenges, or touches me about becoming a better teacher can sometimes be summed up in a sentiment, a phrase, or a few sentences.

Over my years of teaching (for more than twenty years I've told myself that I am half-way to becoming a good teacher; the longer I teach—the more I feel as if I am half-way there), I have developed certain quirkinesses, personal policies, and particular habits of practice. I will spare you the stories of "the why" for each of these habits, ways, and procedures. Suffice it to say, these are the practices and behaviors that serve my sensitivities and limitations. These guidelines are not rigid dogma or laws. They are personal moorings that keep my values true in my relationships with students and allow me to feel like I can hold the space of teaching for which I am responsible. I offer them not to suggest anyone else should adopt one or all. Instead, I offer them as encouragement for your own reflection and list making.

These are a few of my personal policies:

1. It's better to be strict in the beginning of the course, then lenient as the semester progresses, than lenient in the beginning and strict at the end.

2. Be intentional about the use of silences, of pauses, of whispering—there is great power in the silences.
3. Don't teach while tired; don't teach while angry; don't teach while sleepy; don't teach while sick.
4. Be funny—humor in class helps.
5. Teach after having listened to what students say they want to learn; learn to hear what students are meaning when they say what they want to learn.
6. Tell stories about my mother, her mother, and her mother in class to invoke ancestral assistance.
7. Routinely, invite two or three students into a closer vantage point of my work through being teaching assistants, research assistants—having a posse is good for you and them and other students.
8. It's not enough to be engaging and participatory—find ways to be genuine and authentic in classroom interactions.
9. Resist grade inflation.
10. Require assignments be turned in on time; enforce the penalty for lateness. Return the graded assignments the week after they are handed in; if assignments are returned later, apologize.
11. Watch the breathing of students on the first day of class; the longer students hold their breath, the more challenged they will be in trusting throughout the semester.
12. Smile in class; be happy to be performing your job—have fun teaching.
13. Notice the shoes worn by the students and listen to the stories the shoes tell.
14. Work at being trustworthy so that when you must give a negative critique the student trusts your judgment.
15. Know that the fear which is free-floating in your classroom is likely yours as much as theirs.
16. Learn to distinguish between a lazy student and a student who is trying his/her best but not succeeding.
17. If everything that is is not visible, then teach as if the invisible matters.

In a moment of checking with my research assistant, Janine Carambot, to see if she thought a blog about personal policies was interesting, I asked her to write a list of my personal policies as she experienced them in my classroom as an MDiv student. Without seeing my list, this is what Janine wrote:

1. You encourage students to spend time with the question. You insist that the better questions to ask are "What if . . ." and/or open-ended questions that provoke imagination and wonder by the answerer.
2. You refuse sugarcoating the hard things.
3. You seem to be learning with us; you ask us questions and then say "interesting . . ." when we answer; it is a mutual experience for you.
4. You tell us that we need to ask questions for which we do not know the answer—this is a new experience in learning and faith.
5. You do not waste time with "niceness."
6. You encourage us to go deeper when we try to give shallow "churchy" answers.
7. You enable us without giving us answers—you believe the answers depend on context and our social location.
8. You have a way of creating assignments that always beg clarification, but they seem to be intentionally evasive, so you get our own interpretation, creativity, and immersion of the assignment.
9. You have a sense of humor about the things that we tend to take so seriously as if our life depended on it (mostly our theology). If we were able to laugh with you, it was because we saw the limits of our understanding; if we were offended, it meant that we didn't want to learn or we felt threatened.
10. You busted open all our understandings to "educational ministries" by showing us it is not just "Sunday school or Bible study" but something deeper that would seek to overcome the insidiousness of the "-isms." You tell us from the beginning that your classes are "not about education programs in church but about cultivating for the church's ministry and mission in the world and using education as a tool for healing and liberation." This is different than anything we expected. Your teaching is made of the things that we didn't know we needed or wanted—but we discovered that we did, and we do.

11. You bring your own voice and creativity into our classes that help us learn in a way that is a blend of scholarship, tradition, "otherness," and poetry.

Thank you, Janine, I am humbled to be known.

FOR REFLECTION . . .

1. Look back over the two lists mentioned above. Star (*) the ones that you think are important for your own teaching.
2. Now follow suit, list seven to ten of your own personal policies for classes.
3. Ask a student who has studied with you for several courses to create a list of the policies you have performed.

27

Frequently Asked Questions About Courses

A COMMON ASPECT OF websites is "Frequently Asked Questions." This is a handy feature. It is meant to assist the inquiring person with succinct information. It is meant to answer questions searchers did not know they have or provide answers to questions for which they have specific interest. It is also a way for the business to be able to articulate, in a concise way, their benefits, capacities, and capabilities. The key to FAQ is that they are not the questions of the business, but they are the questions of the client to the business. The value is that the business has answers to these distinct and important questions.

I do not want to push this metaphor too far.

I do not think our students are our clients, customers, nor benefactors.

At the same time, I do think that it is important for us, in introductory course preparation, to take on an empathic perspective for our students. We must consider, from their perspective, that they are learning new language, new concepts, never-exposed-to ideas. We must anticipate a version of their FAQ.

Teachers must take time to think through, reflect upon, and design succinct articulation of the benefits, functions, and qualities so that introductory courses are not perfunctory, stale, or unintelligible. Learners should not have to wait until the completion of the degree before they can understand and meaningfully interpret the introductory syllabus.

Below is a list of reflection questions with learners' FAQ in mind. Of course, this is not an exhaustive list of their questions. This list is meant to spark conversation so colleagues, in context, can discuss, compare and contrast, and consider what is better/best for their own introductory courses and the students who trust us with their learning.

ONE: WHAT IS THE INTENTION OF THIS INTRODUCTORY COURSE?

This might be the most difficult of all their questions. If you cannot say the thesis of the course WITHOUT jargony words or technical language or theoretical phrases for which the students have yet to be exposed or taught, then the course is not yet ready to be taught.

For your introductory course, what is the punch line, thesis statement, refrain, big idea? Please write in language that can be understood before the study of the course material.

From the student's perspective, what am I about to be graded about?

TWO: WHAT IS THE APPROACH OF THE COURSE?

The information age is eroding the notion of one supremacist perspective for teaching the big questions of life and scholarship. Unmistakably, there are major shifts in the academy for including multiple voices and many worldviews, even starting with introductory courses. Ideas in introductory courses are no longer "obvious" or "natural" or "to be expected under the circumstances"—a kind of "of course" attitude or "everyone knows" posture as if there is no need for deliberation or new planning or thinking anew.

The question of scholarly approach is in story. In the course, whose story are the learners being asked to enter into? And if not their own story—then why not? What cultural assumptions and presuppositions are operative in the framing of the introductory course? To what are you asking me (the learner) to open my mind, and how will this benefit the people who have sacrificed for me to be a student?

What student skills, practices, and habits will I need to be successful? What new skills will you expose me to for my learning?

The more racial, cultural, ethnic, and age diversity of your learners, the more complex the response must become. Remember that complexity does not have to lead to convolution.

THREE: WHY DOES THIS COURSE MATTER?

The question of relevance is a critical question to learners. The question is sometimes pragmatic and sometimes political—always on their minds.

What do you expect students to become or do as a result of the course?

How much time will it likely take before students learn, change, grow in this material—weeks, months, years?

The question of relevance will shift with the demographics of your students. The more diverse your students, the more complex the response to this question must become. There can be, if we grapple well, elegance in complexity.

The question of relevance is directly related to teaching anecdotes to miseducation. This will be particularly vital for majority culture students.

FOUR: WHAT IS THE VOCABULARY OF THE COURSE?

In the first session of my introductory courses, I got in the habit of initiating a conversation about vocabulary. As part of rehearsing the syllabus, I would tell my students that during the semester I would teach them words that, at first, would feel awkward in their mouths. I told them we would be using a language and jargon that would not work at church potlucks or cocktail parties. But I told them, as learned people, we have a vocabulary in which they must become proficient, even fluent.

The presence of students who speak many languages learning alongside students who speak only one language makes this question more complex.

FIVE: HOW? HOW WILL STUDENTS LEARN? HOW WILL STUDENTS PASS THIS COURSE?

What will I be asked to do to learn?

What will be the task of my body while learning? Am I just to sit and listen as you talk? What student skills, practices, and habits will I need to be successful?

What new skills, practices, and habits will you teach me to engage my learning in this course? What will there be to see, smell, taste, hear, feel—to intuit?

Will there be field trips, excursions, people to meet, new places and encounters where I welcome the stranger and make them my friend? Will I have the opportunity to be as a stranger in hopes of being welcomed?

The educational formation that brought students to college, graduate school, and seminary will have shaped, formed, or deformed learners. Awareness of and attention to students' previous experiences of coursework are critical to answering this question. If there is a diversity of students, e.g., international students and minoritized students, this question becomes much more complex.

SIX: TEACHER—WHO ARE YOU?

We know that many minoritized students learn better when they relate well to the teacher. For them/us, learning is communal and relational. For many majority culture students, the attitude, opinions, and affirmations of teachers are less important and play a lesser role in their achievement.

For BIPOC faculty, all students will likely wonder or question the credentials, institutional value, and authority of those instructors. The identity politics in classrooms is often dangerous for BIPOC faculty, so knowing what and what not to disclose is complicated.

We know from Parker Palmer, noted teacher and author, that we teach who we are.

SEVEN: WHO IS THE LEARNER?

What does it take to design an introductory course before meeting the students on the first day of class?

What can be known about the enrolled students for better course planning?

What are the fears of the learners? By what course design and strategy will you quiet their fears early on in the course?

The more diverse the student body, the more difficult and complicated an answer to this question will be.

Who in your institution is tasked with providing a profile of each incoming class and a summary report of each enrolled student's previous experiences and exposures to learning?

EIGHT: HOW IS THE TEACHER'S PASSION TAUGHT IN THE INTRODUCTION COURSE? IF NOT—WHY NOT?

I have heard senior scholars say that they do NOT teach what interests them until they teach upper-level seminars because they believe introductory courses are not meant to reflect one's own research interests, passions, or professional curiosities. From my perspective, this is wrong-headed and explains, a bit, why some introductory courses are so dull and insipid. How will your passions, unique knowledges, and scholarly know-how be the cornerstone of your introductory course?

Answering these questions does not create a syllabus. And I am not suggesting you add a section to your syllabus for "frequently asked questions." These questions, as a combination, assortment, and hodgepodge, are meant to encourage your planning, preparation, and thoughtfulness to create empathy with and compassion for adult learners who dare to enter into classrooms of religion and theology. Our students, from the very beginning, deserve teachers who are ready and know how to invite them to learn. Learners want courses that are shared endeavors and not just the presence of a subject expert who has not considered the broader experience of their learning.

FOR REFLECTION . . .

1. You may want to remember this list of questions as you are working on a syllabus for an introductory course. Many of them are also very appropriate for any course.
2. Now take some time to look at an introductory course you are teaching or will be teaching, and work through the list of questions for that course.
3. If you are examining this chapter in a small group, look together at these questions:
   - Three: Why does this course matter?
   - Seven: Who is the learner?

28

Creative Bravery

Have you ever asked a question in class for which you did not know the answer; a question for which you did not have THE one answer in mind? Have you ever planned an assignment or designed a learning activity that was so freewheeling that you did not know what was going to happen? What kind of teaching requires the teacher to be comfortable not knowing what will happen next or ever? I suspect it is teaching that is attentive to the personalities, dreams, capabilities, fears, and know-how of each student in particular and the entire class as a whole. Knowledge of each student allows for learning activities, group assignments, selected reading materials, and course aims that are sophisticated, risky, and precisely designed for the times at hand and the diverse contexts in which the students must be prepared to lead.

My hunch is that we too typically create assignments for which the answers and outcomes are forecastable because we have not taken the time to know who is in our classroom. We have specific ideas, standards, and quantifiers for the student to "get it right" with little understanding of the student's individual life experience or knowledge base. Students in turn, while navigating the current educational system, are brilliant at analyzing each professor's wants, then giving that and only that. Professors' quirks are a text that is read, understood, and traversed as much or more as the content materials of our courses. Hallway gossip and faculty reputations assure us that adult students are experts at studying the grading habits and personality types of teachers. In other words, teachers teach with strict disciplinary maps and scripts—a strict adherence to formulaic curriculum—a kind of one-size-fits-all students. The questions and the answers are charted out and planned before gathering with students. Students strain as much to learn the formula of the prescribed script as they do to learn the content of the script. They ask, "Is this going to be on the test?" They say, silently or out loud, "Just tell me what you want me to tell you back." Students learn the ways of gaming the system better than they learn the content of our courses.

What if our prescribed assignments are a detriment to our students' ability to be effective in the workforce? What if scripted outcomes serve only to further domesticate learners? What if the lack of open-ended exploration champions mediocrity rather than excellence?

I suspect it will take creative bravery to reshape, rethink, and reconceive our classrooms. And not just creative bravery in general, but bravery that prioritizes learning our students, their uniquenesses and their potentials. The good news is that creative bravery is commonplace among artists and people who understand creativity as a way of life. The challenging news is that this kind of bravery is suspect and punished in the current educational system.

A clip that went viral on social media depicted the ritual of an elementary school teacher meeting his students each morning at the doorway of their classroom. The daily ritual was to shake hands with each student each morning. Each student had a unique handshake for greeting the teacher, and the teacher knew the unique handshake for each student. Some of the handshakes were simple—one or two gestures. Other handshakes were complex—looking more like a dance between student and teacher than a traditional handshake. It was clear to me that this kind of welcoming communicated to each student that he/she/they were seen and known by the teacher. This was a powerful expression of a teacher who understood the necessity of each student feeling their distinctiveness, being in relationship with the teacher, and knowing they were seen. When students feel seen, known, and welcomed in classrooms, learning improves, deepens, and becomes more meaningful.

The myth of teaching for one-size-fits-all is possibly the worst practice of our teaching craft. We must grapple with finding ways to identify and honor that which each student brings into the classroom because each brings uniqueness. In a jazz band, no one expects all the musicians to play the same instrument—that would be ridiculous. No one criticizes the drummer for drumming or the saxophone player for playing the sax. Each musician is expected, required even, to bring what they have in the way that they have it, in their own voice. Each instrument is required to make the sound of that instrument. Consider, then, that each student should be expected to bring their unique voice and particular understanding to the collective composition of the classroom and that the teacher must welcome all the different kinds of voices. Creativity requires diversity. The band leader's job is not to strip the musician of their uniqueness or their sound, but to blend, sculpt, highlight, spotlight, and listen. The leader's job is to know the many voices and create ways of showcasing each potential contribution.

There is an intimacy that occurs between learner and professor that only happens in the relationship of teaching. It is a profound experience to be seen by a respected teacher and told that, as a learner, you have what it takes. These relationships are potentially life giving and life changing. These relationships are not formed when classrooms operate on a factory mentality where student needs are relatively inconsequential to the teaching. The intimacy shared between teacher and learner makes vivid the humanity of each. Classrooms are spaces where the vulnerability and openness of the adult learner can be met with hope, empowerment, reinvigoration of curiosity, and healing imagination.

This pedagogical intimacy was made vivid to me the first time I read a letter of recommendation written for me by my graduate school professor, advisor, and mentor. The letter described many of the attributes and capabilities I knew I possessed. It also discussed his vision for my potential, my promise, my likely successes as a scholar and religious leader. Much of the budding possibility that he described I was unaware of. And, until reading his letter, I was unaware that he had seen me so well. My mentor, for the three years of study, had paid attention to me in our courses and as I worked as a research assistant. This letter humbled me and set an expectation for which I have been striving.

In contrast, as a reader of applications for jobs, grants, or other high-level projects, I have read letters of recommendation that demonstrate the writer has no passion or knowledge of the applicant. The letter is perfunctory—a kind of mechanical formula that might fit any person who sat through a course and for whom, now, there is an obligation for recommendation based upon an exemplary grade. I have read the same prose in a letter submitted by one recommender for two different people (oopsie!). The writer of the letter did not get to know the student and cannot earnestly recommend the applicant. Many awards have been denied based upon the weakness of a flimsy recommendation by a person who wrote a one-size-fits-all recommendation. If we do not get to know our students, we cannot recommend them for anything.

What would be needed to get to know students who are enrolled in your course before planning the course? What exercises might you plan for the first weeks of a course that would enable you to see, feel, and hear the potentials of our students so that lesson planning might be more precise? What learning activities can be tailored to the uniquenesses of each student? What would it mean to plan a syllabus that can be refined as students become more vivid to you throughout the semester? What kinds of community activities will need to be designed for those who entered degree programs during the quarantine, resulting in only being known through online mediums? If you are teaching huge classes, what strategies will enable you to get to know students?

The risk of getting to know our students is, I suspect, well worth it.

FOR REFLECTION . . .

1. For the current class, describe in a paragraph the students who are in the course.
2. Now look at course goals. Assess how these course goals are impacting the students you described. Are there any readings, class sessions, or assignments that you need to change or adjust?
3. Look at a first assignment you received in a class. Think about how the students in fact fulfilled that assignment. Then reflect on yourself as a teacher—did it take "creative bravery" to (re)shape, (re)think, (re)conceive the assignment?
4. How do your faculty colleagues support you in prioritizing "learning our students, their uniquenesses, and their potentials"?

29

Teaching the Not Visible

My grandmother used to speak in adages, parables, metaphors, similes, and symbols. Now I call her proclivity for language, literature, and meaning-making "wisdom-speak." When I was a child, I thought she was being corny. She knew her wisdom-speak was meant to teach me enough until I am ready to know more.

Her adages came from Bible verses, poetry lines, and quotes from novels, cultural remembrances, and living life as an African American woman in the United States, born in 1887. Folks like Langston Hughes, Booker T. Washington, Sojourner Truth, Pearl Bailey, Jesus, and Sarah Vaughn were regularly invoked.

Wisdom-speak is colorful, witty language—easy to recall and recite, with a depth of multiple meanings. Wisdom-speak is part of everyday conversation. It is a pithy quote or well-placed refrain woven into a conversation like Tabasco on fried fish. It is accompanied by a "hmm" or tongue click, a foot pat, a shoulder shrug or an eye roll. Wisdom-speak is a body, mind, and spirit lesson.

Grandmother Vyola would say, "All that is is not visible." As a child, I thought she meant that there is more to creation than what can be witnessed with the naked eye. If knowing is only about what is directly in front of us—then we miss so very much of all that is. Learning to see the invisible is the task of knowing. Learning the ways of the wind and the saints, angels, ancestors, cherubim, and seraphim; the dream world and the daydreaming world; the ways of prayer and meditation are the learning of the invisible.

Then as a young adult, I decided she was talking about identity politics and the politics of domination. The genderless politics of patriarchy, with its racist undertones and dictates, considers much of "all that is" to be too much for women, many children, and most men. The truncation of imagination engineered by systems of domination and control renders the capacity of many people as inferior, thus negating all that is. Poverty drastically limits opportunities for in-depth exploration—so when we meet persons who have carved out an education in the wake of social depravity, we should be in awe. As a young adult, I came to understand good teaching meant finding ways of seeing the manifestations of oppression in my own classrooms, church, society, and world.

When I encountered Alice Walker, I figured Grandmother Vyola was talking about what Dr. Walker was talking about. Grandmother Vyola is resonant with novelist-poet Alice Walker's four-part definition of a "Womanist" from *In Search of Our Mothers' Gardens: Womanist Prose*. The first part of the definition reads in part, "wanting to know more and in greater depth than is considered 'good' for one."[1] It appears Vyola and Alice were cut from the same cloth.

In the last few days, I have turned my attention exclusively toward preparation for school. I have my head down as I put finishing touches on my syllabi, design learning activities, schedule guest colleagues, locate films, and order art supplies. My mode is one of efficiency and my mood is closed off. I am, in my planning, working from an attitude of indubitability. I have a clarity about what I will teach, how I will teach, and what my students will learn.

While immersed in my preparations, Grandmother whispered in my ear. Grandmother Vyola says that patent planning is not good for me or my students. She advises that the better way is to be more open ended—like Jesus' parables. Allow the students' voice to affect most aspects of the course design, not just the convenient parts. Consider that you cannot see all there is to see, so leave room for your own learning while you teach. Most of all, plan that what is revealed will be marvelous and know it is unplannable but can be readied for. Simply put—get ready!

I have learned to pause when Grandmother speaks. I take a second look at my plans and see that I have relied, a bit, on stale redundancy and a few too many current conventions. I recognize that when I start telling myself I know what will happen, what can happen in my own classroom—I am

1. Walker, *In Search of Our Mothers' Gardens*, xi.

in danger of not allowing for surprise, the unexpected, or the un-expectable activity of Spirit. My grandmothers Vyola and Alice remind me that my certainty is likely a trap. If I plan for only what I know, only what I can see, only for what I can do—then I am not being womanist, not acknowledging all that is in the world.

School starts the week before Labor Day—I am less certain of my plans and better for it.

FOR REFLECTION . . .

Consider a class you are currently teaching or plan to teach next semester.

1. How do you attend to, or make room for, surprises? What surprises do you think might be encountered in the class?
2. Clarify how you are involving freedoms of learning for students. How are their questioning, curiosity, and concerns being integrated into the full length of the course?
3. Whose help (living or dead) do you call upon while designing a course that prioritizes students?

30

Body, Politics, and Love

My teaching goals reflect my expectations that my students will change the world. I want my students to have profound consciousness of love, of themselves as capable beings, of the beauty of creation. I want to instill them with the necessity to fight for the oppressed, uplift the downtrodden, and conspire with the voiceless for a place in the societal decision-making. I want them to be cunning enough to avoid the shallow passions of those who would exploit their talents, squander doing good, and misuse their power. I want them to be wise. With these ideals in mind, I design into every syllabus the notion of the body.

There are few things that are more sacred and more political than the human body. Intentionally engaging the body to learn, while simultaneously making the politics of the body part of the course conversation, is a critical way to get to my lofty teaching aims and kindle my student's passions. Wisdom depends on the body.

A metric I use to assess in-class learning activities is the degree to which I have engaged all the senses of the body in a semester. If, by the end of the semester, I have not engaged all the senses multiple times and in multiple ways, I deem my cache of learning activities for that course as weak. When I engage all the senses multiple times throughout the semester, I notice students' depth of understanding is higher. I carefully design activities for seeing, smelling, touching, hearing, and feeling, not because of students' varied learning styles, but because a multisensory encounter is more interesting and is more satisfying to the curiosity. Giving adults permission and opportunity to learn with their bodies is an act of resistance against the current body politics, which would deem the body only as a commodity. And it's more fun than just sitting still.

I am well versed in shaping courses that point to and analyze the ugliness of the hegemonic politics. A notion that oftentimes intrigues my students while studying the politics of the body in the United States is the ways our bodies are used as indicators of inferiority and superiority. It is thought that to gaze upon a body, one can determine who is male, white, straight, and wealthy. Continuing, it is also thought that to gaze upon a body one can determine who is female, not white, not straight, disabled, and poor. This delusion is perpetuated by the bad science portrayed on some TV shows. There is an episode of *CSI* where the coroner, while investigating a crime scene, uses a caliper to measure the width of the nose of a charred body and informs the detectives that the deceased victim was African American. Disputing this kind of ignorance about the body and race/gender/class/sexual identity politics is the stuff of marvelous classroom discussions.

This semester I wanted to shape a course and a conversation that was a teaching of love, self-worth, dignity, acceptance, and belonging for the personal body, for bodies of knowledge, and communities as bodies of persons. The course is entitled Reading Deeply. I selected one book for us to read for an entire semester. The book we are ruminating over is *Remnants: A Memoir of Spirit, Activism, and Mothering* by Rosemarie Freeney Harding with Rachel Elizabeth Harding. It is a multi-genre memoir that vividly demonstrates an integrated life of deep spirituality and activism. I want my students to be exposed to the wisdom of this text in hopes that they will emulate this wisdom. A thematic thread in the memoir is of healing, wellness, and care for the body.

Pressing students to deeper engage body/identity politics, the first assignment is to create a wellness plan and fulfill that plan throughout the semester. Students reported in about their plan last week. While each woman was making her report (all the students are women), the other students listened with remarkable tenderness. There was an air of respect and regard as each woman told us of the focus of her plan, the rationale for the focus, and the activities she would pursue over the semester for healing, fitness, balance, and rest. The projects were about living into their best selves by disrupting the patterns of ignoring, abusing, or neglecting their bodies. The plans included stopping some habits and starting new habits. In all cases the women were excited about being given course space to consider her own body and contemplate the question "Do you want to be well?" Asking students to live into the principles of our reading rather than just "think about" the reading is their preference for learning. Their reporting felt reverent. At the end of the semester, they will report in again telling the story of attempts at self-care and healing.

The political is always personal. In studying the harm, violence, and inhumanity of identity politics it feels right, needed, even provocative, to teach students to value their own bodies, to respect the enfleshed. The power of love to create a more humane world undoubtedly includes care of self, nurture of body—a tending to the soul.

In the memoir, Rosemarie recounts the words of her mother after recovering from a near-death experience:

> "Listen, Rose. When you die, there is nothing, nothing there but love. Everything else is gone."
>
> "Hmm." I listened.
>
> "Nothing but love," she said again. "So while we're in this world, we have to do whatever we can to love people, to love this world, to take care of all that's in this world. Because that's all that matters, the love."
>
> I closed my eyes briefly. The impact of my mother's words made me sway ever so slightly where I sat. "Hmm."
>
> She was ready to get into bed. She was pulling the covers over her shoulders when she said it to me again, "Now don't forget, Rose. There's nothing left but love. That's the most important thing. That's what you need to know."[1]

FOR REFLECTION . . .

1. Listen to your own body. In any classroom you are a body encountering other bodies. What do students see and experience when they see you? How are these assets for learning for them?
2. Thinking about a particular course, how does that class engender "a conversation that was a teaching of love, self-worth, dignity, acceptance, and belonging for the personal body, for bodies of knowledge, and communities as bodies of persons"?

1. Harding with Harding, *Remnants*, 39–40.

31

When a Course Is Tanking

If you teach long enough, you will teach a course that feels flat, has low morale, or even fails. While a totally ruined course is rare, there are moments when the sinking, the malaise—yours and that of the students—happens. We all know this experience.

If you have never taught a course that has tanked, then you have likely been a student in a course that has. No real need to recount or describe all the ways a course can fail—the ways a course can "go south" are legion. The more important emphasis is to know that when a course is collapsing it can be rescued. When you feel the course sinking . . .

Do not blame yourself.
Do not blame the students.
Do not blame the administration.
Do not blame your family.
Do not blame your pets.
Do not blame the moon phase.
Do not blame the state of the nation.
Do not blame the national economy.
Do not blame climate change.

Blaming is ineffective. Finding fault, placing fault, shaming, guilting, or scapegoating rarely corrects the problem. Sinking courses are not saved through blame.

Do not ignore the situation or pretend that, without adjustment, it will mend. If you sense that there is trouble with the course, the students know there is trouble with the course. When you find yourself watching the clock during your own class session—this is a clue that something needs to be adjusted, altered, changed.

Resist the impulse to knuckle down, grin and bear it.

Resist the impulse to stay the course, stick to your guns!

Resist the impulse to "right-fight" and believe whatever you planned, how you planned, is best and "be damned!" anyone who will not comply with your plans.

Consider that rescuing a course might take a multi-pronged approach. The recovery of the course might need support from others. Don't be a hero—please ask for help. If you feel as if the course is weak, ask for help. If you feel lost or disoriented, ask for help. If you do not know how you feel or what to do, ask for help.

WHAT HELP?

- Get a new perspective, fresh eyes, a more seasoned approach, an empathetic listener. Talk to colleagues. Talk with a trusted colleague at your school, or a trusted colleague beyond your school. You might talk just once, or you might talk several times. Describe the incident or incidents and ask them to listen to what might be changed to strengthen the course.
- Consider asking a trusted colleague to observe your teaching and then assist you with reflection. These talks are not for confessing to being an imposter. Resist reducing these conversations to disclosing your deep-seated anxieties about public performance (save that for your therapist). Use these conversations to troubleshoot, problem solve, and strategize for better teaching and strengthening of your course design.
- Consider, at the beginning of the semester, creating a small reflection group of colleagues (three or four people) for a semester-long conversation so when the course feels like it is not going well you have established conversation partners. The group might be organized around studying teaching resources together.
- Talk with a trusted student to get feedback. Talk with a small group of students and ask their opinion. Perhaps, take class time to ask the entire class for feedback and suggestions.

- Talk to human resource personnel, consult the faculty handbook, know your Title IX procedures. Sometimes bullying behaviors are the culprit in troubled classroom environments.

WHAT MIGHT BE NEEDED?

- Consider that you might need to recast elements of the syllabus. Consider creating different assignments, adjusting timelines, subtracting some readings or adding new kinds of readings. Add a field trip. Invite a guest speaker.
- Ask yourself about yourself. Are you too tired to teach well? Are you bored in your own course? Are you anxious? Are you distracted? Are you disappointed, grieving, or just sad? Do you have an experience of belonging in your institution and in your own classroom? Your vibe radiates to the students and permeates all aspects of the course.
- Are the materials in the course too advanced for the students or too inconsequential? Are the materials culturally aligned and relevant to the students' experiences and expectations? What story are you inviting the students into—is it a story of their imaginations and aspirations?
- What are the larger happenings of the school, community, region, and country that are affecting your classroom? What would it mean to weave these happenings into the conversation?
- Perhaps it is the students—by which I mean, perhaps you do not know the students and their lives well enough. In what ways can you get better acquainted with your students? Do your students come to class tired after a long day of work? Are your morning students tired after having worked all night? Are they taking too many courses? If they are rested, are they hungry while in your class? Awareness of the conditions of your students might help with addressing some of the malaise.

Do not be surprised when a course tanks. It happens to the best of teachers. When a course is "not going well," do not abandon it or your students. Learn, by experience, how to adjust and adapt to create a meaningful experience for your learners and for yourself.

FOR REFLECTION . . .

1. From experience, list indicators of a course that is tanking. Be specific.
2. Using that list, what have you done or what can you do to recover the course?
3. Who can you call for help before the course tanks, so if the course tanks you know who to call? List one or two helpful people.

32

Teaching One on One

It was the first morning of my vacation. The restaurant at the resort had a waiting list for breakfast patrons. The hostess took my phone number and said I would be called when a table opened. I thanked her and walked to find a comfortable spot in which to wait. Not far from the dining room, guests could choose to linger in any of three adjoining rooms—the bar, lobby, or library.

I chose to wait in the library. The room was ringed with mahogany shelves carefully adorned with books and creative objects. Statues, framed paintings, and board games were on display. The room reminded me of magazine covers from *Architectural Digest* or *Good Housekeeping*. The many chairs and couches were positioned to invite guests to linger in small groups, or to simply sit and read. I picked a chair facing the wall of windows. The windows provided a view of the sprawling pasture setting. I noticed a Scrabble board was set on a table near the windows and a chess game was set at another table near the entry door. I, indeed, felt as if I was visiting a friend or relative's home.

As I waited, not because they were loud or intrusive, I overheard a grandfather teaching his grandson to play chess. The boy was about six or seven years old. With the grandfather seated on one side of the board and the boy kneeling in the chair on the other side, the granddad invited the boy to make the first move. As they played, the grandfather patiently explained the way the boy might move varying pieces. Several times, he encouraged the boy to consider a strategy. At the end of the game, the grandfather showed the boy how to reset the board for the next people who might want to play. I overheard the grandfather say he had taught his daughter, the grandson's mother, how to play chess when she was about the same age as the boy.

Even when I am on vacation, I am thinking about and identifying teaching moments. This tender teaching moment between grandfather and grandson was poignant, delicate, and beautiful. It was not extraordinary. Its beauty was in the ordinary occasion of a grandfather taking time, one on one, to play with his grandson.

Some of the best, most tender, teaching occurs one on one.

Classrooms can be marvelous arenas for superb teaching. Classrooms can be sites where the relationship between instructors and learners transforms. Equally ripe with possibility and beauty are the one-on-one relationships between faculty and students that happen beyond the classroom. Teaching students in one-on-one modes has the potential to assist students in ways that the classroom encounter cannot. The opportunity of a sustained conversation with one student can sometimes lead to a long-lasting, life-changing connection.

While I was on a faculty, with intention, as part of my teaching agenda, each year I chose to work with a student teaching assistant (TA) and a student research assistant (RA). I considered these relationships with students as key to my teaching responsibility as the courses I taught in classrooms.

My practice was to meet weekly with each of the two students to facilitate our prescribed tasks. Then, once a month, if the students were interested, I would convene them for a meal to discuss larger theological issues, hear how they were managing in the day-to-day reality of graduate school life, and encourage conversation about their occupational aspirations and dreams. My aim for these one-on-one relationships was to aid their health and success.

I honed my listening skills by teaching one on one. Spending time in one-on-one conversations allowed my primary focus to be on the questions, curiosities, abilities, and perspectives of the student. These one-on-one relationships allowed me to make stronger recommendations for further graduate study or employment options, or give my opinion about life's unexpected twists and turns. A regular dimension of this kind of teaching was when I was able to write very considerate, in-depth letters of recommendation for my students because I knew the student as a person and not just as a student who had done well in my class. Occasionally, if there was trouble, my relationship with the TA or RA allowed for convincing intervention or advocacy.

My practice of intentionally constructing ways of working one on one with students comes from my own experiences in graduate school. When I was in graduate school, the professors for whom I was their TA and RA became my career-long mentors and friends. The three faculty people whom I worked closest with in graduate school have been influential in guiding my entire academic career.

Recently, I referred one of my current mentees to my mentor for guidance on an issue of which he had expertise. I told my mentee that I was putting them in touch with their "grand-mentor."

Through these connections I know I am a better teacher and colleague. Last week, a mentee who serves on a university faculty and just received tenure called me and asked me to talk with one of their doctoral students. I was delighted to assist. Just like grandfather was so glad to teach grandson, I am overjoyed to reach out and support a student of my student.

FOR REFLECTION . . .

1. Think about a teaching mentor that is important for you. What did they offer you in the mentor relationship?
2. How did they mentor? Were there regular practices?
3. What practices of mentorship have you learned, and do you practice?
4. Thinking about your current teaching, how do you work one on one with a teaching assistant?
5. If you are leading a guided study for students, note how you are listening to the students' concerns; note how you are bringing yourself to the conversation.

33

Winter Surprise to Bolster and Brighten

Gray.

The fog, thick and dreary, descended in late December. In early January, the arctic blast assaulted with negative temperatures prolonged over consecutive days.

Unrelenting gray.

Consuming gray.

Days of gray have now turned into weeks of gray. Relief from ice and snow has come in the form of days of downpouring rains—with temperatures still below freezing. Today, the expected high is 36 degrees Fahrenheit, that feels like 32 degrees Fahrenheit, with continued dense fog and forecasted 80 percent chance of precipitation tomorrow. It has been a prolonged—too long—moment of melancholy—dull, grim, and bleak.

Then it happened . . . a few days ago, I received a text from a beloved friend that read,

> Hi Lynne, I accidentally had a book sent to your house. It's called [title of book]. I've read it before, a borrow from the library. It's pretty . . . wild. But you may like it. Hope you like it. [Red Heart Emoji]

Surprise!

Suddenly, the gloom was challenged by a bit of intrigue. A surprise book, an accidental book, was coming to my door. I needed a surprise book, especially if it was "wild." Sure enough, that day the delivery person dropped the book on my porch. Immediately, I started reading. Immediately, I discovered a new author. Immediately, my spirits lifted.

There is something about surprise—when it is pleasant—that combats the dreariness of the season. A surprise can chase the blues away or at least make the blues melodic and survivable.

Teaching in the dead of winter can sometimes mean teaching in prolonged frigid weather. Winter can be both real and metaphoric to describe our environments. We know that our bodies, minds, spirits react with and are affected by light, temperature, barometric pressure, and precipitations. Being mindful of your own mood and the moods of your students is part of classroom management and good teaching practices. Consider, when the moods are gray, planning a surprise.

Too often planned surprises in courses are punitive—like surprise quizzes or surprise tests. That is not what I am talking about. I am talking about surprises that delight, intrigue, and bring some welcome relief from the long, too long, winter.

When I received the marvelous book surprise from my friend, I was reminded of the ways I would attend to my own blue moods while teaching. I recalled some of the ways I would make gestures to bolster my students' moods in the middle of the winter. I would, for them and for me, change the tempo of the course, introduce something or someone unexpected, and nurture a lighter-hearted atmosphere. Somehow, and most times, these gestures of care shifted us for the better.

Here are a few examples of ways I went about changing pace and surprising my students:

- Brought a basket of chocolate to class to be passed; enough chocolate for all to have much.
- Planned a spontaneous change of venue—I moved the class session to the library, to the gym, to a science lab, or to a lobby of the building to sit on couches.
- Invited a surprise guest lecturer; lecturer was the author of the book being read; former student who had done well in the course; local celebrity; dean, provost, or president to discuss the topic of the course.
- Planned a potluck or moved to the refectory for class—shared a meal during the class.

- On a few occasions I brought my collie dog named Max to class. He was a warm and gentle giant who, as students arrived in the room, happily greeted those who wanted to play, then Max laid down at the door and slept until break when he received more pets and cuddles. Max's presence lifted many spirits of students, and their glee made me smile.
- On several occasions, I thought of a class session as being like the "Free Parking" space in a monopoly game. Rather than what was planned for that session, I invited students to gather up their thoughts, questions, concerns, and we discussed whatever they wanted to discuss. Anything that came up! My conversation prompt would be: Where are you in this learning? What have you learned thus far?
- I would suspend the planned session and gather students around (change in seating pattern) and ask them So what? / Now what? questions. I would ask, How do you make meaning of this newly glimpsed perspective or new concepts? How does this affect your thinking, being, doing? What does your community, family, tribe think of what we are discussing? Is any of this valuable to your community?
- Brought art supplies to class and invited students, rather than taking notes, to draw, color, sketch, or work with play dough throughout the lecture.
- Shifted to a skill-based lesson. What skills have you noticed that students do not possess, but you need them to be able to do? For example, good student skills of reading comprehension, writing skills, questioning skills.
- Showed a film complete with popcorn, soda, and candies.
- Read aloud children's books, poetry, or short stories.

You get the idea. Please be mindful that I am not saying for you to do what I did.

Your context is different than mine and your teaching landscape is not mine. My point is to encourage and invite you to be aware of your own wintertime mood and the wintertime mood of your students, then adjust, modify—meet your students where they are, as they are.

In the wintertime, sometimes the gloominess is better survived with a change of pace, with a gesture of care and warmth, with an acknowledgment that we need to be with one another but in gentler ways. If/when you can brighten the spirits of your students, your own spirit will be glad.

Winter will give way to spring. We teach in hope.

FOR REFLECTION . . .

1. Look again at the lists of surprises above. Which have you practiced in your classes? Remember these are surprises that "delight, intrigue, and bring some welcome relief from the long, too long, winter."
2. Now thinking about yourself; think about a surprise that has come in the last two months that has impacted your teaching. In what ways?

34

Don't Stigmatize Failure

JUST THE THOUGHT OF FAILURE, either in anticipation or in loathsome memory, causes many to recoil, wrench in pain, or feel ashamed. The big, red-inked F on the exam, either literal or metaphorical, sends chills down spines and contracts sphincters. Fiasco, disaster, confirmed lack, or found-out mediocrity humiliates and destroys.

Failure is unavoidable. As they say, "We learn more from our failures than from our successes." Rather than stigmatizing those who fail, it behooves us to embrace those who are brave enough to make attempts and normalize the help needed to strengthen efforts. Still, normalized help is not easy to come by.

For many students, for many reasons, one of the first things they do in undergraduate or graduate school is fail. A student who excelled in high school courses will not necessarily ace the first exams in college. Comparable to students, teacher failures are as varied as teachers. Early career fiascoes, mid-career blunders, late career mistakes, and poor judgments—confirm that we are persons who are fallible. Humanness is messy.

Our teaching failures remind us that an expert in any field does not necessarily make for a good teacher of that field. Learning to teach the methods, approaches, practices, and literature of any discipline requires as much attention as learning the content of that field. Any seasoned teacher will tell you that there were (many) failures along the way to becoming a competent teacher.

The ways schools respond to failure is a key element in the formation or deformation offered in our educational enterprise. Students and faculty are more formed by the ways they are accepted or rejected during failure as they are by any course in the curriculum. A climate of help, support, applauding persistence, and reward for courage tells students if they are worthy of the degree they are attempting to earn. It tells teachers that the community where they teach has their backs.

Higher education colleagues report that they survived an educational process that told them that failures were to be rare/never and were intolerable. Out of self-protection, many of us learned to pretend we do not fail. Or we have been taught to hide the failure. We masquerade or just never quite own up to any failure. School ecologies that are intolerant of failure are climates that are deforming of spirit and shallowing of imagination. Without healthy spirit and deep imagination, education becomes rote, wooden and hollow. Our students, then, are ill equipped to leave our classrooms.

Calvin Coolidge said,

> Nothing in this world can take the place of persistence. Talent will not; nothing is more common than unsuccessful [wo]men with talent. Genius will not; unrewarded genius is almost a proverb. Education will not; the world is full of educated derelicts. Persistence and determination alone are omnipotent. The slogan Press On! has solved and always will solve the problems of the human race.[1]

In classrooms, it behooves us not to lower standards, inflate grades, or dumb down curriculum so there is little to no failure, but instead create ecologies of learning where moving past failure is integral to learning, encounter, discovery, boundary expansion, and new experiences. Asking for help is not cheating; it is not a show of weakness; it is not a declaration of permanent inadequacy or insufficiency. Failure does not foster mediocrity or create indelible flaws. Asking for help is difficult. Asking for help must be re-learned.

I first met Ariel as a student enrolled in my introductory class. His habit was to sit quietly, listen attentively, and participate actively in small group activities. I noticed that he was smart when I read his first submitted essay. His writing was strong, his grasp of the course material was solid, and his conjectures concerning implications and applications was superb. By midterm of the semester, Ariel's engagement in the class showed that he was, consistently, a capable and talented student.

1. Coolidge, "Press On!"

During a break in a class session Ariel came up to me to talk. He said he had a proposal. I was intrigued and listened attentively. His proposal was that since he had done so well on the first three writing assignments, that I would allow him to forego the remaining three assignments. I told him to let me think about it. At the end of class I pulled him aside to talk. I told him that for me to forego the three pending writing assignments, he would have to agree to help students in the course who were struggling. I told him he would not have to do the remaining assignments in the syllabus, but instead he would use his time to lead a study group to help failing students. He said he would think about it. During the following week he emailed me and said he would take my offer. I emailed back and told him to meet me in my office an hour before our next class.

Before the next class and my meeting with Ariel, I emailed three other students who were also doing quite well in the course and offered them the same deal. If they were willing to keep up with the reading of the course, in lieu of writing the remaining three essays, the four of them would help other students who were struggling with the materials.

When we met, I told them that their help with other students was not mandatory and they could complete the course as outlined in the syllabus. Each chose to create a study group with other students. The study groups worked well; help was given and grades came up.

After the last class session Ariel came to my office. He thanked me for the class then said, jokingly, that the deal I struck was unfair. I smiled at him and waited to hear his rationale. He said that the task of creating the study group, and helping other students, was much more work than had he simply written the remaining essays. I smiled wryly and reminded him that it had been his choice. I asked him if he had learned from helping. He said yes. I told him that there were students who he helped who would not have taken help from anyone else. And I thanked him for his good help. Ariel told me I owed him lunch. Gladly, I obliged.

Winston S. Churchill is thought to have said, "Success is stumbling from failure to failure with no loss of enthusiasm." So, we ask these reflection and invitational questions. To whom do you turn for help with your teaching failures? What systems of help do you build into your courses for your students? In your school, is there an ecology that normalizes failure and regularizes help, support, and resilience, and if not, what would it take to create one? Who are your collaborators and conversation partners when you fail and when you need help? What failures in teaching are weighing you down and need to be forgiven and healed?

FOR REFLECTION . . .

Thinking about ourselves and our teaching, choose any of the questions and note how you respond.

1. To whom do you turn for help with your teaching failures?
2. What systems of help do you build into your courses for your students?
3. In your school, is there an ecology that normalizes failure and regularizes help, support, and resilience, and if not, what would it take to create one?
4. Who are your collaborators and conversation partners when you fail and when you need help?
5. What failures in teaching are weighing you down and need to be forgiven and healed?

35

A Rant About Safe Space

PLEASE INDULGE THIS LOW-GRADE RANT. I believe the notion of "safe space" in adult classrooms is un-interrogated and oversubscribed. The question is . . . Safe for whom?

Well-intentioned teachers, in wanting students to attempt deep conversation, wrongly presume adult students need to feel safe to effectively learn. Rarely is it asked, What does it mean if the conditions that provide safety for some are the same conditions that render others vulnerable and exposed? I believe safety, as a proviso for student participation in difficult conversations, is potentially harmful for societally minoritized persons and potentially counterproductive to the aim of critical engagement for all.

Of course, classrooms need to be spaces that are free of abuse, assault, and bullying of learner and teacher, alike. Severe breaches in civility, blatant acts of hostility, and covert violence are monitored by institutional policies and procedures for human rights. The notion of safe space, as I understand it, does not attempt to guard against those encounters regulated by institutional protocols for human rights. Instead, the notion of safe space proffers itself as creating space for conversation among persons with differing interests, opinions, and worldviews. Suppose safety for the comfort of some students is made at the expense of other students?

Never have I attempted to achieve safe space in my own classrooms. Unfortunately, I have participated in conversations when "safe space" was declared by the facilitator or participant. The declaration is usually without discussion or explanation of what "safe" means in that ecology. In the classroom, when someone proclaims "This is safe space," then all are expected to follow suit with this ambiguous contract of engagement. Too often, safe space is foisted upon the group without definition or consensus. This defies best practices of learner-centered classrooms.

Secondly, as I understand it, safe space is usually characterized with the inference of confidentiality. In declaring safe space, participants are encouraged to speak openly and honestly of their thoughts and feelings because in safe space, allegedly, words will not be repeated beyond the room. Certainly, no one, given the choice, wants to feel vulnerable while doing the hard work of learning or teaching. Rather than encouraging students to build courage, hone the skills of listening, and develop a more thoughtful approach to ideas and their power, declarations of safe space lull participants into reckless disclosures of sensitive details of their lives. If students or teachers think that what they say will not be repeated simply because of declared "safe space," then there is a lack of awareness of human frailty and sin. After all, what happens in Vegas NEVER stays in Vegas! Additionally, it feels foolhardy to suggest the therapeutic tool of confidentiality as responsibly operational in a classroom setting that does not have the expertise necessary for a therapeutic approach to dialogue. Religion and theological classrooms are never appropriate places for therapy.

Thirdly, safe space seems to imply people who risk speaking have the promise of no accountability. Persons are instructed that they can speak honestly, openly—as if the lure of safety will bolster the confidence of the shy or the weak. Problematically, safe space views conflict and behaviors of consternation as bad and to be avoided in classrooms. This politically correct attitude unwisely implies that everyone has the right and privilege to feel safe everywhere. Built into this cavalier vagueness is the presumption that judgment is suspend-able during the discussion—meaning words have no binding, communal consequences for the person who speaks them. Detaching the words from the person who speaks is the politic of Western, supremacist thought. Disembodying the spoken words from the one who speaks feels counterproductive to embodied, liberative pedagogies.

Finally, those with privilege—inherited, granted, or snatched—exercise few coping skills for feelings of vulnerability and powerlessness in adult classroom spaces. The notion of safe space is initiated when those who are unaccustomed to being vulnerable are pushed beyond their norms of experience. Safe space, then, leaves those with societal targets on our backs (women, LGBTQ, economically disenfranchised, non-white, etc.) to listen to those in power who now, in safe space, can speak with reckless abandon. The speaker, shrouded in safety, naively and insensitively escalates to sentiments that too often spring from narrowness of experience and ignorance of the ruthless politics of body and oppression. The wounding, jagged politics of gender, sexual orientation, class, and race are exacerbated in safe space. Safe space primarily serves to create comfy hotbeds of spoken bias and arrogance that potentially demean, brutalize, and belittle those who are expected to listen in the vacuum of safety.

FOR REFLECTION . . .

1. What do you now think when you hear the phrase "safe space"?
2. What kind of atmosphere of community and learning do you seek to shape in your classes?
3. Looking at one of your classes, list four or five or the key risks students are taking by enrolling in it.
4. We do have responsibilities to create spaces where students are free to express themselves, where they can take risks, where they can be supported, where they can learn. How do you seek to build this environment of community and learning in your class?
5. How do you assist students to find support when they encounter the risks in your classes?

PART FOUR

Practices—Ways of Teaching

In what ways do we shape classes to guide, inspire, or affect learning? How do we craft learning activities, discussions, and assignments to enhance learning? In what ways do we inspire independent learning and collaborative learning? How do I know what learning has occurred? How do I empower students?

36

Partnership

Dissuading Rugged Individualism

EXPOSING AND DISRUPTING THE values that perpetuate white normativity puts a strain on the adult classroom. Individualism is a cornerstone value of whiteness and patriarchy. As persons committed to the flimsy lie of pulling oneself up by the bootstraps, too many students believe that education is best attempted alone. Conforming to the principles and practices of individualism, adult students believe that by leaving the people who formed and shaped them they can better demonstrate excellence. By denouncing accountability to and responsibility for their people, their kin, and their community, they are becoming good US citizens. "To thine own self be true" is exaggerated to narcissism, isolation, and dangerous detachment. The exceptionalist values of this US society teach that to be real you must be alone.

Equally, the US educational system functions to uphold the societal tenets of individualism. Higher education rewards individualism. My teaching colleagues were told that the only way to make a legitimate contribution to their scholarly field of study was to do it alone. Collaboration is cheating! We are discouraged from playing well with one another. Consequently, teachers typically insist upon and praise individualism in adult classrooms.

Even for students who understand themselves to be part of a community and enabled by the sacrifices of others, adult classrooms are places of disorientation. The new perspectives, new expectations, new experiences, and new ideas challenge even the most prepared, supported, and grounded student. For the student who presumes that individualism is the best way to approach study, the disorientation can become severe and can make learning terrifying. The hardcore pledge to individualism that is a hallmark of US society and the academy only serves to exacerbate the student's anxieties.

Further confusing to the adult student steeped in the delusion of individualism is the classroom that values partnership, cooperation, and collaboration. Group assignments and shared projects that are designed as counterpoints or correctives to society's hegemonic imagination dumbfound the student who believes the better way is the autonomous way. I have heard loud and painful groans when students, upon reading my syllabus, understand that group work is part of the course experience.

Students who believe their work is best showcased in isolation resist and refuse to work on group projects. On more than one occasion, I have had to disband fighting groups. On a few occasions, groups were crippled by the logistics of when and how to meet. Repeatedly, groups will do tandem reports with each person giving individualized speeches rather than working for a synergized, harmonized product. In several instances, I am certain that groups relinquished power to one student who then did most, if not all, of the work. In all these situations, my hunch is that those students who saw no pedagogical value in collaboration sabotaged the groups. When self-reliance eclipses a sense of community, belonging, and mutuality, or when self-reliance is at the expense of communal care and responsibility, then classroom spaces that affirm values of mutuality and teamwork become experiences of deep pain and confounding for the students—and the teacher.

I want my students to become aware that knowing is communal and that learning is relational. Individual knowledge is a fallacy. How we make meaning depends upon the context(s) in which we find ourselves. Who we are and whose we are has direct bearing upon how we learn as well as the measure and merit of learning. Knowing and knowing better requires awareness of relationships. Individualism limits, constrains, and distorts efforts to know beyond yourself.

Over the years I have developed strategies to signal to students that their connection to their people while learning is paramount and that my classroom is a place to develop skills for collaboration, partnership, and cooperation. The exercises are not meant to instantly dissuade students of individualism as a core value. They are meant as moments to consider that there are other, maybe more generative, values to hold dear while learning and living.

One of my learning activities is a ritual of invocation. Early in the semester I ask students to consider people, living or dead, who would be glad they are enrolled in my class. I tell them to think about people who would support them in school when things get difficult or people who have their best interest at heart as they move through coursework. When students are ready, I ask that each student in turn speak aloud the full name of one of the people. I instruct students, saying one name per turn, to exhaust their list of people. Once all the names have been spoken, I acknowledge the ancestral and communal love in the room. This conjuring often sustains us.

Another exercise is a reflection activity. I give students time to think through their answers, then instruct them to write their answers as succinct lists on the blackboard:

- Who are your people (describe in race, class, gender and other social location indicators)? To whom are you accountable while in this degree program? Who is praying for you while you are here? Who do you struggle not to disappoint as you study?
- What highest job of leadership will be afforded you once you have demonstrated reasonable mastery?
- What is the suffering of your people? What are their vulnerabilities? What is their trouble?
- Which aspects of their suffering and anguish will you bring to bear upon the conversations in this course? How will you work so that with the taking of this degree you are more informed about the needs of your people?
- During your studies, in which systemic oppression will you become expert for the healing of your people?

These kinds of learning exercises help reconnect and remind us we are not alone. At least they help me. Each time I do an exercise of this kind, I name my own ancestors, the babies yet to be born, and our troubles. I, too, am reminded that I do not teach alone and that I do not teach in vain.

FOR REFLECTION . . .

1. Think about how activities of collaboration in your academic work, guild meetings, or faculty meetings have enriched or strengthened your scholarship/teaching. What activities have been particularly helpful to you? Focus on the helpful ones.
2. Now translate that reflection to your classes. What strategies for collaboration have you used in class settings? Which work best for you?
3. Note how these could be enhanced. How do you prepare students to work together? How do you supervise their work? How do you grade this work? How do you let them help you grade it?

37

Learner-Centered Teaching

JUSTICE IS ONE OF those ideas that has captured our imaginations for generation upon generation; yet it is still a contested notion. Collectively, systemic racism, sexism, classism, homophobia, white supremacy, and a judicial system that is lenient on "white collar/white male" crime, while vengeful upon the poor and minoritized people, provide ample evidence that justice for some is not justice for all. For these and other reasons, I need my students to be articulate about the notion of justice. It is not enough to "believe in" the idea. It is not enough to agree with it intuitively or "in your heart."

Education as a practice of freedom, as a practice of transgression, as a practice of re-humanization, is the praxis I teach in my graduate level introductory course. This course insists that the ability to articulate the theories of justice, regardless of personal experience or personal belief, is a pedagogical necessity.

It is the rare student who enters my introductory course able to speak the language of liberative pedagogy or to talk about the connection between education and social transformation. This is why they are learners—there are important things that they do not yet know and that they cannot articulate, but that we can teach them.

My pedagogy of justice is not so interested in teaching skills of "critical thinking." Most of my students have families, are gainfully employed, and have responsibilities in church as well as community. Many own their own businesses, provide support for several generations in and beyond their households, and are looking to religious leadership as a second or even third career. By the time they reach my Introduction to Educational Ministries course they have demonstrated considerable ability to think critically, to problem solve, to engage successfully in tactics of survival.

Rather than "critical thinking," I want to teach my adult learners methods of power analysis necessary for the summoning of moral courage in a society steeped in body politics, violence, and systemic hatreds. I want my students to be praxis thinkers, able to analyze injustice and articulate justice in an unjust society. They must be able, in their own communal context, to analyze white supremacy and patriarchy in its myriad expressions. The healing of their community and the restructuring for a more equitable society depends upon their ability to articulate justice. What I stress in my course is the ability to articulate what justice entails in the world. Simply feeling it, believing it, desiring it, hoping for it—just won't do. The power is in speaking it.

Have you ever known something but could not articulate it? You thought you understood it, but did not know the words, the vocabulary, the way to convey the basic concepts with depth? Sometimes, as a consequence of complex experiences, you may find your ability to describe the learnings of that experience to be limited or incomplete. In order to give full voice to your experience, as well as the insights gained from that experience, drawing on the collaborative power that emerges from sustained conversations is key. Equally, having a firm grasp upon basic theories of justice making and moral courage are imperative. Being able to articulate theories of justice provides a hermeneutical mirror for analysis of and meaning-making from personal experiences and perspectives.

Finding ways to assist my students with articulating theory and helping them order the learnings of personal experience entails exposure to new vocabulary and interrogation of basic concepts. Personal experience can provide new insights, new understanding of the age-old problem of injustice when communal-reflexive habits are incorporated to animate and elucidate theory. Because, of course, theory and practice are two sides of the same coin.

On the first day of the course, then reinforced in each subsequent session, I tell my students to pay attention to the argument of the authors we are reading. The focus of reading is not so much deciding if they "like it or not," but noticing the authors' use of vocabulary, basic concepts, and illustrative examples and narratives. I tell them to learn these funky words and use them in and out of class.

Once new vocabulary is mastered, the ability to conceive the basic concepts and the ways these concepts create the theory is more evident. I tell them to be able to map the basic concepts of the theory because all basic concepts do not function in the same way to create the theory. When they look puzzled, I teach them concept mapping. Learning to play with theory for praxis is a mighty challenge. I have, over the many years, devised this midterm learning exercise to assist my students in articulating the basic concepts of the theory we study:

Step One: I email, before the class session, and instruct my students to be able to access in class all the readings, all their notes taken, and all the assignments graded thus far. In other words, bring all your stuff!

Step Two: Once we are gathered in class, I tell them to get out all their materials and base any group participation upon our conversation since day one of our class. In other words, do not talk off the top of your head; focus upon what we have been discussing all semester.

Step Three: I divide the class into small groups. I inform the groups they have an hour to collaboratively write ten basic concepts of the theory of liberative pedagogy. When the anxiety in the room spikes, I remind them that they are to use all the materials they brought to class. Sometimes the anxiety lowers and sometimes not.

Step Four: I say, "On your mark—GO!" I do not tell them it is a midterm exam, but it is.

Step Five: While the groups are working to articulate their lists of basic concepts, my teaching assistant sets up the computer so there is a blank page projected on the screen for all to see. The teaching assistant, during the report in by the small groups, will record each of the concepts I approve to be written on our class list.

Step Six: After the hour, I reconvene the groups for our "round-robin report in." Our aim is to take the lists from all the groups and create one list of basic concepts that we can ratify as a class. We refine the concepts during the group report in through our conversation and through my editing.

A member from one of the small groups reads aloud one basic concept from the list they created when it is their turn. Groups will have multiple turns but will report in only one concept at a time. If, when the one concept is shared aloud, the concept sounds reasonable and resonates with our collective understanding (and my listening ear), then the teaching assistant records the draft of the concept as read for all to see.

Once that concept is typed on the screen, I ask if any other group has a similar concept. If so, we use the other group's work to wordsmith the concept on the screen until it is clear and strong. If not, we wordsmith as a class.

Once a concept is refined to my satisfaction, we move to the next group to read aloud the next basic concept from their list. We continue with the "round-robin report in" until all the groups have exhausted all the concepts they recorded during their small group collaboration and until we have one common and sound list of basic concepts. This takes about an hour.

Step Seven: Then, I provide a list of basic concepts from a previous course as a final way to strengthen our collective work. I invite the class to look through the list to add, reword, or strengthen the new list we have just drafted. There are always additions, edits, and rewordings to strengthen the list we have just created. Students like seeing the work of other classes as it lets them know the complexity of the task of articulation.

Step Eight: I ask, referring to our list on the screen, "Does this list of basic concepts articulate the theory we are studying?" If yes, we celebrate our hard work. If no, we continue to work until we are satisfied with our articulation of basic concepts of emancipatory pedagogy.

Step Nine: I email our list of basic concepts to each student. Of course, my students' ability to excel at this exercise varies from class to class. Most fascinating is that, from year to year, no two lists of basic concepts have ever been the same while still capturing the crux of the theory. Every class has found their own way of articulating, from their own unique perspectives and experiences, the basic concepts. I am not looking for an essentialist or universal list of basic concepts. I am looking for their rendition.

We say a learner-centered education nurtures, kindles, and coaxes students into voice. With voice comes the responsibility of agency and service. Teaching toward voiced students is teaching the ability to speak articulately, eloquently, and intelligently about the issues of oppression, hegemony, violence, and captivity—and not just passionately, without substance. Coming into voice is hindered by class sessions riddled with self-centered, pseudo-psychological moments of students filibustering through personal stories and anecdotes. Learner-centered teaching focuses upon the learner being able to articulate new ideas, new theories, new concepts, new vocabulary, and hopefully, newly refined visions for a more just and equitable society.

FOR REFLECTION . . .

1. Make use of, or adapt, the midterm process for your own classroom. By midterm, can students articulate the basic concepts of the theory being taught in the course?
2. What value is there in creating a midterm "exam" that is open-book and collaborative?
3. Audit a course design and determine how new vocabulary is introduced, defined, and practiced. What support are students given to assist with incorporating new vocabulary into their thinking, writing, and learning activities?

38

Writing a Lecture / Writing an Obituary

RECENTLY, MY BURDEN, CHALLENGE, and task was to write my father's obituary.

Obituaries typically allow eight hundred to twelve hundred words to depict and describe a person's entire life. As a writer, this was a daunting task. As a daughter, it was impossible. How to proceed? After reading the obituaries of other family and friends—noting their style and form—I decided my challenge was to cover my father's ninety years on planet Earth by giving facts and data. I wrote and then checked the accuracy of dates and spelling. The draft read like a file for a candidate for the witness protection program.

I scrapped that version and launched into version 2. I soon stopped myself.

My flowery prose and long sentences sounded like a rejected Hallmark card.

Finally, I sat and considered my father and those who were mourning him. In this time of homegoing and celebration of life, what did I want to assure my family and community about my father? I decided, with resolute conviction, that I would write Lloyd R. Westfield was a noble man—because he was. The final obituary emphasized his courage, strength, and fortitude of care and concern—all traits of nobility. I told people about his life-long journey as a musician, special education teacher, school psychologist, fraternity member, and churchman. Mostly, I wrote about his passion for his family and for our African American community, and the many ways his love was steadfast.

I wrote a good obituary—one that described my daddy as a man who was earnest, dignified, generous, and loving. I knew I was writing a narrative that rarely appears in racist America about Black fathers, yet it is a story that was my everyday, family experience. I wrote his obituary as a gesture of resistance against the distorted portrayals that slot all Black men into a few flimsy, stereotypic categories assigned to them. Writing Daddy Lloyd's obituary was an act of compassion for the unnamed African American men whose stories of unwavering commitment to their families is unappreciated, overlooked, or ignored.

Writing Dad's obituary has made me consider how I write lectures. I do not often lecture in my courses, but when I do, how do I write what I write? Do I give the data and basic concepts, and then expect students to resonate with cold facts? Do I tell them "my version / my answer" to the question at hand without considering their perspectives, contexts, and situations? Do I spend time choosing vernacular that will invite them into deeper thought and heightened resonance, or simply rely upon the stilted, obsequious vocabulary of the religious academy? Do I lecture to my students the same way I would lecture to colleagues, and then wonder why students are lacking understanding when, in fact, it is my communication skills that are subpar?

Relying upon facts and data as lecture material is thwarted by the adage "Content is cheap." In the digital age, students have as much or more access to data than the person who is lecturing. It is commonplace for Siri and Google to know more facts with greater accuracy than the person lecturing and for students to consult Siri and several search engines during the lecture. Learning to write lectures that resist multiple uncontextualized definitions, lists of statistics, and block quotes is a challenge worth attempting. The challenge is to design a lecture whose argument is not based upon a contrived or universalist understanding. We must lecture to demonstrate and expose our own modes of epistemological creativity and scholarly meanderings. In other words, lectures are more valuable to students if they are works of art rather than mundane spreadsheets set to words.

Writing a good lecture takes time, as it is as much engineering and architecture as it is poetry, prose, and story—a complex enterprise, indeed. My best lectures are those that have been given several times and have the benefit of reconsideration and rewriting after questions, answers, conversation with my students. Like my father's obituary, any topic warranting the writing of a lecture will be much too large and expansive to be satisfied by one lecture. It behooves the writer to contemplate the needs of the students who will hear, witness, and glean from the lecture. Clarity about the viewpoint of the lecture is as important, or more important, than writing the thesis statement for the lecture. Students do not want the delusion of neutrality; they want to hear your opinion, consider your "take," and then have the opportunity to resonate and align or disagree, question and debate. Good lectures are evocative, provocative, and able to bring complexity to the learning journey without befuddling the learners.

When I consider the better/best lectures I have heard, the lecturer has exposed, claimed, and shared their own thinking rather than hiding behind a mask of noncommittal to the material at hand. The lecturer made their own social location clear in the stance they took, rather than claiming some kind of generic identity or essentialism to the work. And the lecturer worked at the craft of words, which helped me know what they were saying while they were saying it. Dense materials can be lectured, but the words to convey the density must be carefully chosen so the listeners, the students, can hear and access the materials. This is not a dumbing-down of material. This is the craft of writing in such a way that there is flow, synergy, and wide thresholds of encounter and discovery. Listeners must be able to see the pieces as well as the whole of a lecture.

I suppose it is possible to elevate a poorly written lecture into a good lecture by the way it is performed; however, most of us cannot rely on our performance. Drawing the listener in, locating them in new worlds, challenging them to new perspectives, providing a previously unconsidered rationale—this is the work of a well-written lecture. We must not doubt that students are seeking disruption of, and a counternarrative to, the hegemonic imagination that has been revealed as moral bankruptcy at this moment in history. As I have learned from my beloved teacher Katie Geneva Cannon, the best lectures seek to debunk, unmask, and disentangle so students might have the wherewithal to change the world toward justice.

Writing an obituary is not easy. Writing a lecture is not easy. Each, in its own way, asks that we not ignore the tender fragility of our souls, but speak our souls into the room. Each written piece is the work of healing—for us and them. The writing is simultaneously truth-telling, soul speaking, and hegemony-challenging. I exhort you not to write lectures or obituaries if your goals are any less.

FOR REFLECTION . . .

1. Think about lectures you write for / use in classes. Consider editing long lectures down and adding stories, questions, conversations, meditations, or reflections. Would this improve students' ability to learn?
2. Think about what the key purposes for your lectures are.
3. Think about how students respond to your lectures; think about student behavior during your lectures.
4. Now look at the questions asked above about how you/I prepare lectures:
   a. Do you give the data and basic concepts? How do you sort through what is important in a lecture?
   b. Do you tell students "your version / my answer" to the question/topic?
   c. How do you connect with or include their perspectives, contexts, and situations?
   d. What is the "vernacular" of the lecture? Does it invite students into deeper thought and heightened resonance? Does it introduce them to the vocabulary of the religious academy?
5. Finally, think about some of the most helpful lectures you have heard. What made them "helpful"?

39

The Intent of Discussion

IN A LOW AND pensive voice, the young woman student posed her question to the all-women course. Her question sent a gentle shockwave through the room. After some far-ranging discussion, my response to her question was this: "Black women all over the world make passionate love all night long, and then in the morning, go to their jobs looking fabulous!" I admit that I had never previously had this kind discussion in a classroom, but I was intrigued. I was, with this conversation, in uncharted territory in my own classroom discussion—and loving every moment of it!

There are reasons, good reasons, why discussion is not a preferable learning activity in higher education. Teachers know from experience that discussion leans toward the will and want of the student. Discussions can, and do, "get out of hand." Discussions can move into territory not on the syllabus or beyond the scope of expertise of the teacher. Methods to control and orchestrate classroom conversation are in all our teaching repertoires.

We must resist thinking of the moments of questions after a lecture as "discussion." A question posed and then a response is not a conversation. Q&A is not discussion.

As a professor in a seminary, it has been apparent to me for many years that students come to class with "churchy" agendas and preferring "churchified" discussions. Students are aware of the standards of "acceptable" discussions. Students also have the habit of making a study of the teacher as much or more than they study the topic at hand. In the study of the teacher, the student makes a concerted effort to ask questions and provide responses that are a match to the sensitivities of the teacher. In these instances, the lesson by the learner has more to do with mimicking the masks and personas of the teacher than exposing and plumbing her own curiosity. Some teachers enjoy this gaslighting.

Given the pitfalls and dangerous possibilities, I still work hard to engineer conversations in my classrooms that will be life changing, thought provoking, and courage summoning. Wielding the transformative power of deep conversation is my cautious aim. I want to engineer conversations that evoke astonishment and amazement. I want my students to experience, as I have experienced, conversations that heal, convict, and rescue. I yearn to choreograph conversations that allow students to ask the questions that they are genuinely wondering about, rather than the question they know is acceptable, palatable, and often benign.

When we get it right, discussion can bring a magical kind of encounter resulting in insight, revelation, new perspective. The moments when students listen to and for each other as mutually shared engagement on tough issues is the moment of shared truth and ah-ha! The shared experience, as if something important is being cracked opened, as if some new light is entering in, as if the world expanded a tiny bit, is the result of deep, risky discussion.

For two courses, over the last eighteen years, I have had the good fortune of registration exclusively by women. I had not made a Mary Daly rule for registration, so in both instances, I was surprised and delighted. Each time I have taught an all-women course, I have wanted the exclusive presence of women to be more than a novel classroom experience. I wanted the conversation to be substantively different. I wanted to create space for a conversation by women for women about women. In both courses, once I realized registration was exclusively women, I made changes in the syllabus. I rethought the learning activities and created exercises that considered and honored the all-women group. I changed the readings of the course to exclusively readings of women authors. I shifted the cornerstone questions of the course to consider issues of female identity, femininity, misogyny, misogynoir, and womanist approaches to self, community, and power.

The discussion that evoked my comment about the love-making habits of Black women happened in one of the all-women courses. Our discussion about gender and womanhood was provoked by a new learning activity. I had instructed each woman to create a timeline of her own hair. It was a straightforward and simple exercise that uncorked a mammoth discussion.

For those women whose hair had been a living symbol of maturity, personal growth, and participation in beauty culture—this assignment was a guide for recollection, reminiscing, and reflection. For those women whose hair had been a place of ongoing authentication of imposed inferiority, a constant tethering to a beauty standard that is unyielding in abuse, a site of verification for worthlessness and ugliness, this assignment was fraught with anger, ire, and tales of unhealed wounds.

The political is personal and the personal is political. Discussing the body is a discussion of creating ourselves, including our politics, and has the potential to teach us how to summon moral courage. A discussion about our hair, for women, is potentially a discussion that moves into the arena of authentic reflection on sexism, racism, classism—the politic of superiority and inferiority that permeates the society. Since the body is the site of gender politics, racial politics, class politics, and the politics of sexual identities—it is precisely the body that should be discussed.

I am not saying other professors need to ask students to create a hair timeline. I am suggesting that the tool of discussion in our classrooms warrants our deepest attention if we are to move toward the conversations that are politically necessary for social change and healing. In so doing, I want to suggest that conversations among certain particularities are valuable and necessary yet underutilized in classroom strategies. There is great merit in discussions on race and racism among only white students. There is tremendous benefit for all-male groups to discuss issues of sexism, misogyny, and misogynoir. I am a witness that the all-women conversation in two courses was life-giving.

FOR REFLECTION . . .

1. Note how you use discussion in classes. What is the purpose and hoped for outcome of discussion? For example, are discussions to deepen understanding of class content, are they to provoke thought, are they courage summoning, are they healing? Discussions have many purposes if carefully planned.
2. How do you prepare for a discussion? List the steps of your preparation. What notes/hints/tasks do you have in front of you as you invite a discussion?

3. Thinking about classes you teach: Are there some groups and classes for which discussion is a useful tool? Name them and contrast them from other times you did not think it is as helpful a practice.
4. Reflect on the purpose of discussion listed in this reflection—I want my students to experience, as I have experienced, conversations that heal, convict, and rescue. I yearn to choreograph conversations that allow students to ask the questions that they are genuinely wondering about, rather than the question they know is acceptable, palatable, and often benign. Write a sentence or two about your teaching intents when you incorporate discussion in your courses.

40

Identity Politics

Until It Is Faced

Training students to identify and traverse the identity politics in the United States begins on the first day of my courses. On day one, I introduce myself, then launch into the syllabus review. In describing the required readings, I hold the book or article in my hand, tell students the kind of text it is (fiction, non-fiction, etc.), then I discuss the author. I identify the race and gender of the author and give a description of the author's work in and beyond scholarship. And then I tell the students my rationale for selecting this author and particular text for our conservation.

Last year, during this part of the syllabus rehearsal, a white woman student, whom I will call Sara, raised her hand while I was waxing on about the authors. Sara (age fiftyish, married, middle to upper class, suburban mom of three teenaged children, devoted church member and avid Jets fan, self-identified as politically liberal) asked that I stop identifying the race of the authors. I have paraphrased this interaction in the following vignette:

Sara said, in a chastising tone, "The race of the authors does not matter. We should read the books regardless of the person's race."

I responded, "In our classroom conversation, my race matters, your race matters, and the race of the authors matter. Our voices and our perspectives, our values, our behaviors, and our beliefs are directly connected to our racial identity. No author writes for all people or from a universal perspective. We must be aware of their perspective to better understand their work." Sara looked puzzled.

I continued, "Sara, when you look at my face do you see the face of an African American woman?"

Immediately, Sara looked suspicious. She strained for what to say. She did not know if she should say she saw my race or if she should say she did not see my race.

Sara said, "I don't think of you as a Black person. I think we should just be people." Sara gestured as if she had said something obvious.

In my mind, I heard her say, "I think we all should just be white people . . . normal people . . . just plain people."

I said, "My race informs me and to ignore my race is to ignore my voice, as well as the voices of my people. Please know that I like being an African American woman. I embrace our ways, wit, and wisdom."

Sara's face again became quizzical, like she was considering something new and for the first time. She looked unsure.

I continued, "I think of you as a white woman." This soft statement hit her with a jolt. Sara's shock gave way to dismay—she frowned. Seeing her alarm, I suggested that she hold her concern for later in the semester. I went back to my syllabus rehearsal.

When I entered the classroom for the second session, Sara was seated. As I unpacked my briefcase she came up to talk with me. She reported that while she enjoyed reading the African American woman author bell hooks (our first assigned reading), she did not think hooks was talking to her.

Sara said, "I just think bell hooks has such a different perspective . . . I am not sure why this book is assigned for this class."

I told Sara to "hang in" with the conversation—it was just the beginning.

On the last day of class, as Sara walked out of the door, she thanked me for the "nice" course. Her hollow pleasantry reminded me of the way a tourist, while leaving the tram ride, thanks the guide at the end of the amusement park safari.

I thought of James Baldwin. James Baldwin, acclaimed novelist, legendary essayist, and important human rights champion, said, "Not everything that is faced can be changed, but nothing can be changed until it is faced."[1] I made a mental note to include writings by Baldwin the next time I taught this course.

I love Baldwin's use of the word "faced." It means to confront, challenge, provoke, even threaten or defy. He is also not so subtly suggesting

1. Baldwin, "As Much Truth as One Can Bear," 38.

that people need, if societal change is to be given a chance, to turn and face one another. Baldwin suggests that relationships of respect, decency, decorum, and dignity will change the world for the better, if we have the fortitude, tenacity, and care to make the attempt. The politics of the face is serious territory. The police do not take a mug shot of your feet or elbows. We are known by our faces. We face the world with our faces. Most racial profiling happens in the nanosecond it takes to gaze upon the face. *The Sweat on Their Face: Portraying American Workers*, an exhibit of the National Portrait Gallery at the Smithsonian, says, "The face is the primary canvas of the story of our lives."[2] I agree.

Once Sara signaled on the first day that conversations on social hatred were new to her and that she lacked the experience of challenging the social lies she had internalized, I watched for moments of distress and discomfort through the arc of our semester-long conversation. From my recollection, here are the three teachings that also shook Sara:

(1) Just as victims of rape are not experts in the crime of rape or experts on rapists, so African American people, with our experience of violation, dehumanization, and oppression, are not experts in the sin of racism or the contributing systems of oppression. We are typically, and rightfully so, reactionary. Reactionary is not the same as critically reflective. Please do not expect African American people to inform you about the intricacies of racism. Surviving racism does not equip one to teach about racism. Consult well-informed and mindful white persons who are aware, repentant, and doing the work of equity and justice. There are many people.

(2) Even with the sophistication and technological advancements of the twenty-first century, many white people still do not think they have a race. They still think race is for "othered" people—people of brown-hued skin or simply Black people. Even so, white people typically do not hesitate, on a census form, to tick the box for Caucasian or white. Given the choices of Asian, Hispanic, African American, or mixed, they can declare they are white. Other than selecting that box, the everyday behavior is usually one of tension, anxiety, nervousness, or just plain confusion about issues of race and racial identity. They still believe that their racelessness is just being "normal." The politics of this identity-delusion is debilitating to non-white people.

(3) The United States has exported its systemic prejudices and social hatreds around the world. As an American traveling overseas, being

2. Smithsonian National Portrait Gallery, *Sweat on Their Face*.

African American has mattered sometimes in dangerous and unpleasant ways. Being an African American has made me a novelty in Japan, an oddity in Korea, a target in Jamaica, an object of suspicion in Ireland and Israel, beloved in Ghana, and ogled at in France. The emotional outpouring, from rage to reverence, was at times overwhelming. The world is quite aware of the racist and stereotypical narratives of blackness in the United States and, for the sake of power and prestige, has chosen to embrace them. As an African American traveling abroad, I am often a spectacle, an embodiment of the racist narrative. I was a spectacle as in celebrity or spectacle as in despised—all expressions of objectification, commodification, and all quite scary. Racism in the United States makes it difficult for African Americans to travel the world. It was challenging for Sara to understand that our goal is never to overcome all differences (being post-Obama is not the same as being post-racial), since God clearly created our spectrum of differences. God loves our faces in all their many colors, textures, shapes, and sizes. It is when differences are deemed to be deficiencies that the problem of othering occurs.

When whiteness and maleness are considered "normal," then any person not white and not male is, by base logic, abnormal and inferior. This white supremacist mentality undergirds and maintains social systems that control, sort, are suspicious of, exploit, criminalize, or eradicate (quickly or slowly) those who are deemed as other. Facing this reality is our liberation—mine as well as Sara's.

The Saras of our time are uncomfortable when the lies of the melting pot and assimilation are exposed, countered, and rejected. There is great resistance in allowing the voice of someone who has been othered (bell hooks and me) to speak our perspective. There is surprise, dismay, and disorientation to learn that those who have been othered have a perspective of merit, even a perspective that is potentially revelatory. Allowing another's perspective to decentralize previously uncontested norms, values, and beliefs takes time, prayer, and patience. As we wait, we must acknowledge that until it is faced, we will not be able to find our way forward. I have an urgency about this.

FOR REFLECTION . . .

1. Think about the image of face. For you, does face mean face to face? Does it mean "face into the wind"—the realities around you? Does it mean face into the mirror and describe what you see?
2. Look specifically at one course you are currently teaching. How do you help students face into the class? How do you see and note their faces? How do you help them interact with other faces? "Respect, decency, decorum, and dignity" do change the outcomes when coupled with "fortitude, tenacity, and care."
3. What does it mean in your school's context to acknowledge race and the racial identity of the teacher and student? What aspects of your course design offer reflection on issues of racial identity and body politics?

41

Collaboration

Not for the Faint of Heart

THE PROJECTS HAVE AT times crashed and burned. There have been the occasional minor derailments. In several instances there were irreconcilable differences and un-repairable circumstances. Once I declared utter, dismal failure. On the other hand, there have also been profound insights; reports of experiences of magic and awe—accounts of life-changing and unanticipated learnings. Most of the times, the projects are completed, the aims were gained. The cause for pause is that even with success there is a critical note of feedback from students that suggests the result did not justify the means because of the difficulty, the time consumed, and the demanding nature of the learning methodology. Collaboration is not for the faint of heart.

On the first day of my seminar courses, I routinely give students the opportunity to negotiate a change in the syllabus. This semester, the students negotiated to change the required collaborative assignment to a recommended collaboration. Further, if they choose to collaborate, their dialogue partners could be persons beyond our course enrollment. Their spoken rationale was that collaboration is just too complicated and the logistics were just too demanding. I also suspect they did not want to risk their grade on the strength (or weakness) of a peer's efforts. I honored their request. I sympathized with their reticence. I, too, have had many occasions to collaborate on writing projects, committee work, and administrative tasks. These occasions, whether ultimately successful or not, have been overly time consuming and emotionally draining.

So, I ask this very basic question: If students cannot effectively collaborate in coursework assignments, what will it mean for their abilities to collaborate in employment, family, church, government? The question of collaboration by students leads directly to the question of collaboration by teachers. And then, in answering the question of collaboration by teachers, one must ask about collaboration by administration. This leads to an entire unraveling.

Should students collaborate in course work? Yes and no; only sometimes and hardly ever.

I suspect the question of collaboration would need to be the center of a huge curriculum transformation where the models of theological education are re-thought, re-designed, re-engineered toward community building and relationship tending as primary modes of learning. The curriculum, to be viable, would teach as core values such notions as partnership, coalition building, and the African notion of ubuntu as well as immerse students in models of mutuality in leadership. There would need to be a clear understanding that the curriculum was shaping students into societal change agents for social justice and peace.

Collaboration seems so countercultural to the common motifs of lone ranger, top of the pyramid leadership, and sole proprietorship. US culture prides itself on individualism—"pulling oneself up by one's own bootstraps." Our government has the checks and balances of the many but looks to the one for leadership. Our denominational structures, still bastions of patriarchy, are cautiously measured in their change even in the face of certain institutional death. If divinity students learn from pedagogies of collaboration, will their abilities find resonance in the marketplace of the church and society?

Maybe we do not as much need to teach collaboration as we need to teach negotiation—similar, but different ideas. Donald Trump, like him or not, has become a cultural icon based, in large part, upon his ability to effectively swing a deal. The TV version of Trump does not make vivid the compromise, cooperation, concession, and sacrifice needed to swing the deal. I want students to meet the challenges of working for peace rather than negotiating treaties of war or deals in ministry that are self-serving and opportunistic. Maybe I need to develop course assignments that strengthen students' abilities to negotiate and ask students to report on the compromises, cooperations, and concessions that enabled the deal to have buoyancy—hmm.

I find less and less value in assignments that ask students to sit alone with their own thoughts and write critical essays.

I want students to move toward the enfleshment of notions that allow for penetrating experiences of community, for shalom—the Isaianic notions of the lion and the lamb lying down together. At the same time, I remember Rev. James Forbes, pastor emeritus of The Riverside Church, saying that when the lion and the lamb lie down together—the lamb will be very, very nervous. Hmm . . .

My motto, words from Maria Harris, printed at the bottom of my syllabi reads, "If it is not expressly prohibited, consider it a possibility." Next semester, I am going to expressly prohibit students from renegotiating the collaborative project.

FOR REFLECTION . . .

1. What kinds of rules, structures, or prepared-ness might assist students for deeper, more worthwhile experiences of collaboration in classroom assignments?
2. How would the applicant pool and subsequent matriculating class be affected if admission processes required candidates to critically compare and contrast a successful and a failed attempt at collaboration?
3. Does the digital age rely upon collaboration, i.e., even if use of technology is so often a lone activity, are there overlooked or misunderstood experiences of life in the digital age for which teachers need more understanding and wider critical reflection?

42

Excursions and Pilgrimages

THE LIBERTY BELL. THE Franklin Institute. The Betsy Ross House. The Philadelphia Zoo and Botanical Gardens. The Art Museum (infamous for the Rocky run up the stairs). Boat House Row. The Philadelphia Public Library. My brother and I attended public schools in Philadelphia, and these were some of the places we visited on trip days. These days were marvelous! Each trip brought great anticipation. We were thrilled about going, doing, being outside of the school building and away from the routine of the classroom setting. For each trip our excitement, and the excitement of our classmates, was palpable.

The excitement burst from the classroom into our household. There were permission slips to be signed, brown bag lunches to be packed, and outfits appropriate for the trip to be laid out the night before. Once we returned from the trip, the stories of what happened and what we experienced carried us for days.

Certain people and some kinds of experiences cannot and should not be brought into the classroom confines. Certain knowledge is best encountered in community, in neighborhood, in museums, in parks, and even on rivers and while crossing over oceans. Taking students to new lands, to meet new peoples, to encounter new smells, tastes, sounds, sights, feels, and ideas summons the imagination that is too often dampened in classroom spaces. My hunch is that there are mysteries, experiences, knowledges, and truths that refuse to enter the classroom; these understandings require learners to participate in excursions, pilgrimages, and field trips. In other words, some of the best learning happens outside of the classroom. Learners must leave home to learn.

If done correctly, excursions guarantee a decrease in a teacher's control of learning and an increase in a student's control of learning. Many teachers, for example, have taken learners to the zoo to view the newborn panda only to have little Jane or Johnnie be fascinated by the flock of pigeons and never once pay any attention to the pandas. Pigeons were not on the syllabus and will not be on the test! What if learning resists domestication? What if the better learning does not tame us, but instead makes us wild, unruly, and free? What if, when given the chance, learners set their paths in such a way as to render our established curricular choices as being contrived and unhelpful in the landscape of the twenty-first century?

What if the roads discovered while learning are more interesting than the roads mapped by teachers?

The longer I teach adults, especially scholars, the more I work at giving up control of their learning and allowing them to "go" by themselves into learning experiences. In several classes, I required students to design their own excursions based upon the themes we were studying in my course. Students were instructed not to go anywhere alone; they had to take someone from class or from their family or friends or church members. I requested that the student facilitate a conversation with the accompanying persons and include the comments and impressions (based upon course learning outcomes) of their companions in their excursion report.

Some of the most successful learning of students happened when they went into the world with their teenaged children or their church deacons—going together to places they had not been and talking with people with whom they had previously had no discussions.

I learned from my colleague Heather Elkins that some excursions are pilgrimages. Sometimes, leaving the classroom requires the search for and journey to holiness and wholeness. I have had the privilege of witnessing the movement of the Holy Spirit with my students in New York City, Newark, Maui, Accra, Dublin, and Long Branch, New Jersey. Sometimes we were in a retreat setting—there for an intensive course. And other times we were traveling together for weeks—crossing borders, visiting our global neighbors in their own homes, mosques, and shrines. Pilgrimage learning takes ahold of entire groups and brings expected and unexpected lessons for teachers and learners, alike.

My advice is to resist trying to orchestrate trips that demonstrate the theory you are teaching in class as if the theory is in action in the world. Teaching and learning is much more complicated than this—learning defies this mundane dichotomy. Instead, ask yourself: Which colleagues' work is best encountered, viewed, and metabolized in a visit to their studios, offices, shops, pulpits, and places of business? What trip will best assist students with connecting the knowledge they have with the knowledge they need? What experience will challenge the normative gaze of students and allow them a new vantage point upon the complexity of a craft worth seeing differently and better? Then—design a trip.

Excursions, field trips, and pilgrimages must not become logistical nightmares; teachers are not travel agents nor concierges. And, refrain from trips where the passivity of the classroom is duplicated in the field. Students leaving the classroom to sit in different chairs to hear someone else's lecture is not optimal. Take students, body-mind-soul, into the world so they can encounter the unknown and the previously misconstrued.

My most agile traveling students have always been my international students. I suppose it makes sense. If you are courageous enough to leave home and settle in a new country to learn—going to NYC is welcomed—journeying to learn is your motif. My most fearful students were those who had never traveled on urban public transportation and wanted me to rent a bus from New Jersey to New York so they would not have to bump up against the peoples. I paired the fearful students with the international students and off we went to see what there was to see (via NJ transit and NYC subway). We all survived!

Sometimes, mystery tiptoes around pedagogical mundanity and refuses to reveal its riches until we take or send our students out into the world. Avoid the commonplace and design encounters for your students that will surprise, delight, befuddle, and amaze. What my brother and I remember most about our childhood field trips is that they were days of fun. Learning moved from the daily routine and became enjoyable. Plan experiences for your students and for yourself that bring fun and joy into the collective learning.

FOR REFLECTION . . .

1. Think about a particular class: How might an excursion and a pilgrimage "demonstrate a theory in action in the world"? List three or four excursions that would indeed embody "theory in action."
2. Think about these excursions as pilgrimages: How might you and the class be engaged or changed by the excursion?
3. If the better learning requires leaving the familiar for the unfamiliar, in what ways might these excursions help us encounter the "unfamiliar"?
4. Since we teach adults, where could you send your students to learn and report back about their encounter? What time would you carve out of classroom time for sending students into the world? What would it take to assess their learning of having ventured into the world?

43

A Key Ritual

Our attempts to teach toward openness, toward possibility, toward new glimpses of an uncharted future mean that teaching can be challenging, even confounding. One way I learned to embrace this approach was by incorporating rituals in my course designs.

The use of rituals in classrooms allows students an experience that moves them into realms where meaning-making requires imagination and vision. Rituals can provide provocative and creative ways for students to enter and inhabit course content that otherwise would go overlooked, underinvestigated, or ignored. Rituals create space for learning through intrigue, encounter, and invocation.

Below, I recount a class ritual I designed to coax students into claiming more power, agency, and voice in their own learning. Here is my key ritual.

Ten graduate students and I went to a retreat center by the sea for an intensive four-day course focused on the notions of mystery and imagination. At our first session, we gathered in a large room and sat on folding chairs arranged in a circle. The all-purpose room had a wall of glass windows with views east toward the Atlantic Ocean. From the circle, we could not hear the waves, but we could see the sea stretching out. The afternoon sun gently setting into the horizon was lovely and the perfect backdrop for our key ritual. It was a beautiful place to learn together.

I sat in the circle holding a black bag.

In preparation for the first session, I had collected an assortment of keys. My collection included skeleton keys, hotel room digital keys, metal house keys, roller skate keys, safety deposit box keys, padlock keys, piano keys, house radiator keys, clock keys, keys for maps, a thumb drive with Stevie Wonder's "Songs in the Key of Life"—as many kinds of keys as I could find. The bag was a black and white beaded drawstring purse with a long fringe. I carried the bag when I was in junior high school. When I found the purse in my closet, I was glad I had saved it all these years. All the keys were in the black bag and the black bag was on my lap.

Holding up the bag in front of the class and jingling the bulging bag as I sat, I said over the noise of the clinking contents, using a suspenseful and serious tone of voice, "I am going to bring the bag to each of you. When I come to you, reach into the bag. Select one object. Just one—you cannot handle two!" I chided. "When you pull the object from the bag, this object becomes yours. Its power will become your power. Do not let anyone else view your object. Keep it concealed in your hands. Hold it to your bosom. If you want, glimpse at it through your interlaced fingers or turn your back for a peek. Do not let anyone see your object."

Some students became reticent. Some looked a little hesitant. I was having fun.

I passed around the circle taking the open bag in turn to each student. I held the bag high so the contents of the bag could not be viewed. Each student, following directions, reached into the bag and retrieved an object that was some kind of key. As instructed, students took care not to show their key. Some students used both hands to keep the key from view.

Once everyone had a key I asked, "Before we show what we have chosen, or more to the point, what has chosen us, does anyone want to give back what has been taken from my bag? Does anyone want to return their choice to the bag? Or does anyone want something different from the bag?"

These questions brought a thick, full silence into the circle. I waited for their decisions. Everyone signaled that they wanted to keep what they had chosen.

"Very good, then. You can reveal what is in your hand. You can reveal what has chosen you," I said.

Students unfurled their fingers revealing their gift, revealing their key.

Some looked happy—had smiles on their faces.

Some looked quizzical—had arched eyebrows and squinting eyes.

Others looked confused—looked at their key then around at the keys of the other students as if they had received something strange or questionable.

I continued, "For the duration of our course you will carry your key with you. You will get acquainted with the power of your key. Remember—keys open doors, providing access. Keys also lock doors, providing safety and protection. This key will give you power that you already possess but have not accessed or for which you have not been disciplined. Your key will help you become more of who you already are. With your key you have the power to open and close at your behest. During this class get acquainted with your power and use it wisely."

I instructed that the next step was that each student would take their keys and a notebook to a quiet spot inside or outside of the retreat center. Each person was to find a comfortable and private spot to converse with their key. For an hour, the person will interview their key; contemplate their key; draw their key; write a story, song, or poem with their key in the starring role. Get to know your key and record what your key tells you about its purpose, power, history, and value. To my surprise, these instructions were met with eagerness.

An hour later the group returned to the circle. Each student told a fascinating narrative about what they had learned from and about their keys. The reports included drawings, song lyrics, journal entries, and poetry. Each was beautiful in its own way. For the rest of the course students explored the power of their own agency and imagination and how those attributes were symbolized and animated by their key. At the last session of the course, I brought the drawstring beaded purse back to the circle. I asked if anyone wanted to return their key to the bag. Everyone kept their power.

This is what I learned. When courses are more than spaces where information is memorized, then regurgitated, students who are unacquainted with self-reflection and possess little self-knowledge feel lost or are easily overwhelmed. When classes are spaces of wonder, curiosity, and deep deliberation students must be acquainted with their own power to question. They must be willing to bring their own agendas and to consider a wider way of being. Too many students are unaware of their capabilities and capacities as learners. They are unacquainted with their own genuine.[1] Adult learners who enter classrooms with little self-knowledge are often skittish, suspicious, and ill prepared for the challenges of classroom endeavors. This lack of knowledge makes it difficult to teach. It takes some modicum of self-awareness and clarity of purpose for learners to take hold of courses at a level of depth worth pursuing.

1. Thurman, *Sound of the Genuine*, 12.

Our job as teachers, in part, is to assist students with un-learning the ways that dampen their voices, and that keep them afraid of new learning. We must assist them with re-learning ways of agency for their own pursuits. Sometimes, it takes rituals in teaching to move students past their fears and move them into their power, courage, and commitments. Giving students keys was my way of ritualizing my expectations that they would use their power to learn, to come to voice, to tap into their own desires and yearnings.

FOR REFLECTION . . .

1. What rituals can we lead so that students feel more themselves in our classrooms—i.e., empowered, voiced, and capable?
2. What does it mean to teach toward possibility, and how do rituals make the impossible possible?
3. What rituals assist in creating a learning environment where students learn their own value and worth and dignity?

44

Genuine Inquiry

Mr. Sosnow, my fourth-grade teacher, interrupted the class as we copied our homework assignments into our black-and-white marble composition books from the chalkboard. With a sly look in his eye, Mr. Sosnow informed the class that he had a special homework assignment for us. He instructed us that by tomorrow, we were to find out how air is made.

I ran home, burst through the front door, and blurted out the question as soon as I saw my mother: "Mom! Where does air come from?" She looked puzzled.

She said, "You mean the air we breathe?"

"Yes!" I replied impatiently, "It's our homework assignment." Mom explained that the air we breathe is made by plants. I stopped in my tracks. "Made by plants?????" I asked. She said that it is called photosynthesis. I thought for sure this was one of those rare times when my mother was mistaken. I thought for sure this could not be correct because we had lots of plants in our house and in our yard and I never once saw a plant make any oxygen.

Mom saw my doubt, my disbelief, and my suspicion. She said, "If you don't believe me—look it up." In our house "look it up" meant the Oxford dictionary or our beloved set of World Book Encyclopedias. I ran to the bookshelves and returned to the dining room table with the "E–F" book of the encyclopedia—to look up photosynthesis. My mother informed me I needed the "P" book. I thought if I needed the "P," then surely, she did not know what she was talking about. I would likely, I told myself, have to wait until my dad got home from work—he would know about oxygen since my mom was, clearly, misinformed. My mom sat at the table with me and helped me find photosynthesis in the "P" volume of the encyclopedia. I was amazed! Oxygen comes from plants—it was in the book! I wrote up the findings from my investigation. When my dad got home, I regaled him with my vast knowledge of the way green leaves take carbon dioxide, water, and sunlight and turn them into oxygen.

The next morning Mr. Sosnow created a panel of students to present their findings. Each child, in turn, offered his/her explanation of the production of oxygen. The panel presented several creative and one outlandish notion. I was the final student to speak. I explained photosynthesis and showed a concept map my mom helped me copy from the encyclopedia. At the end of the panel presentations, each student in the class cast a vote for the best explanation of the origin of oxygen. Photosynthesis and I won in a landslide.

The beauty of this fourth-grade learning exercise was that Mr. Sosnow knew his students did not know about photosynthesis. The aim of the assignment was discovery. So often in adult classrooms, teachers pose questions, create learning assignments, and craft assignments for grading that presuppose that our students possess certain kinds of knowledge. But what are adult students supposed to know? And if it is so clear, why do so many learners not know?

So much of the ecology of higher education communicates that learning is for adults who already know. My fear is that students spend more time pretending to know than they do in discovery, investigation, encounter, and wonder. Our adult students have learned to create strategies against being blamed, punished, embarrassed, and shamed for not knowing what they are supposed to already know. Their charade comes in many forms: asking shallow questions at the beginning of the class to get attention in the conversation, belligerent silence during classroom discussions, physically hiding behind computers or, to my personal annoyance, talking over people to prove they know what they do not know. Students will also filibuster or attempt to derail the conversation for a conversation set by their own agenda to exhaust the time of the session. All these behaviors are defensive tactics to survive classrooms where the supposed-to-know knowledge is simply not known. The intense pressure to perform knowing often stifles inquiry.

What knowledge should teachers of adults be able to expect? I can honestly say I do not know. It is the same "I do not know" when asked what kinds of jobs adult learners will have in a society in such flux that current jobs are folding and new jobs are not yet conceived. Education cannot meet the needs of a world that is changing at breakneck speed. The enterprise of education does not know what it is supposed to know—just like our students.

I confess, when I think of what my students do not know, I am, often, judging persons as remedial, miseducated, and under-prepared. If I/we shed our arcane notions of stagnate cognitive standards that are already out of step with the world, focus upon the learner's curiosity, and aim at giving the needed tools for investigation, discovery, and inquiry, perhaps we would, together, create more meaningful learning. Adults who make it into a classroom in higher education know a lot, they know enough. How much trust would it take to work with a student to find out what he/she does not know so learning would be more meaningful? How many discovery assignments are needed to support students who do not know?

In the fourth-grade exercise, I experienced amazement because what I did not know was not held against me. Instead, what I did not know was my point of inquiry and consequently amazement. My successful inquiry convinced me that the world was a mysterious place and a place where the mystery could be interrogated and understood—at least a little bit. I want my adult learners to be amazed as they learn new ideas, as they encounter new perspectives, as they discover the new complexities of old thoughts, beliefs, and traditions—even if the discovery is about what I think is basic.

FOR REFLECTION . . .

1. Think about a particular course you teach. Note the goals, purposes, and learning outcomes for the class. Of course, part of these are encountering center ideas/texts/practices/etc. But more than that, how does the class help students engage in "genuine inquiry"?
2. What assignments help them connect learning to their lives and context?
3. How do assignments help them move from knowing and responding to enacting, interacting, and living?
4. How do the assignments help them move to "discovery, investigation, encounter, and wonder"?
5. Enhance or rewrite one class assignment with "discovery, investigation, encounter, and wonder" in mind.

45

Emotional Responses to Being Graded

THOUGH THIS MEETING OF the Academic Standing Committee was many years ago, my memory of a request as filed by a student yet lingers. Bonnie, not her real name, was petitioning for a grade change from B to A in our required ethics course. In the rationale section of the form, she explained that she would soon be going before the denomination's ordination committee. Her dilemma was about her transcript and its interpretation by the lay committee. Bonnie feared that by having been given a grade of B in Introduction to Ethics she would be misconstrued as being an unethical person. In the petition, Bonnie took great care to assure the faculty committee of her high character and high moral fiber. From my recollection, her writing conveyed a low-grade sense of desperation and shame.

Of course, the committee recognized the confusion of her rationale and elected not to change the grade. A grade in a disciplinary course, even if the course is ethics, is not an assessment of personal decency or moral fiber. Similarly, an academic transcript is not a predictor of vocational success or failure. After the Academic Standing Committee ruled, Bonnie's advisor was asked to talk with her and explain our decision.

My hunch is that the sentiments and fears of Bonnie are more pervasive in students than we would want to think. What are we communicating to students about their personal virtue and value in grading? When a transcript is interpreted by nonacademic persons in authority, in Bonnie's case an ordination committee, are they clear that the grades are not a measure of the goodness of the candidate? What do grades mean to adult learners—many of whom are already highly accomplished in the vocation for which they study?

Once the joys and jitters of the beginning of the semester settle in, I look to the next milestone—the first assignment. The part I enjoy about the first assignment is seeing the work of students up close and personal. The part I dislike about the first assignment is grading. Specifically, I dread returning the graded assignments to students. My difficulty is the emotional response of students about their grades.

Returning graded assignments is a moment when the energies of the room rise and fall, spike and soar higher, then dip, quiver and swirl—all seemingly in simultaneous, mostly silent, drama. Students who receive a "good" grade, usually A, sit looking proud, feeling understood and sometimes smug or condescendingly satisfied. Some students look inquisitive, usually the A- or B+ grades, rereading my comments and trying to make sense out of their "mistakes" or my poor judgment. Students with grades that are below B+ often allow their attention to drift or even pout for the remainder of the session unable to engage with the teacher who obviously is incompetent, misinformed, or downright prejudiced against them. Returning graded assignments is a moment loaded, overloaded, with student emotions, and this moment, for me, has proven many times to be distractingly burdensome.

So many student reactions communicate that if I gave their assignment the highest grade then I "like" them and think they are "good" human beings. And, if I gave their assignments a lower grade, then I "dislike" them and think they are "bad" human beings. I am just as unprepared for the emotions of joy, satisfaction, and pride as I am for the emotions of frustration, disappointment, or anger.

My spiritual practice for this weighty moment has turned to detachment. It is not my wont to disconnect (not to become unattached) from the students nor to dampen their responses. I do not want to shield myself from the emotions of my students. Detachment helps me to maintain my own composure and direction during their emotional highs and lows. I want to keep this moment in perspective as one moment among many throughout our shared experience of learning. I want to resist reacting to their mood with my own mood. The practice of detachment allows me to stay focused on the building of community in the course as well as upon the notion of mutual respect. Detachment, like submitting oneself to be graded in the creation of a transcript, requires hard work, discipline, and commitment.

I have thought of Bonnie many times when I return the first graded assignments in a course. Her heartfelt dilemma reminds me that while grading is not a determiner of character and worth, it is a sensitive experience to which I need to carefully tend.

FOR REFLECTION . . .

1. What is your spiritual/teaching practice when you return class assignments?
2. What do you hope grading accomplishes in the class?
3. Looking at a particular set of assignments, what are the criteria you use for grading? What is most important in your grading?
4. If you list a grading rubric in the syllabus, reread it. How do you affirm it, interpret it, and teach it in class sessions? Are there any ways you could improve it?

46

Teaching Better Reading Habits

In junior high school, we were taught that all the sections of any assigned book were to be read. We were instructed that "good students" never overlook any section of the book. This point was reinforced when the answers to a few critical test questions came from the preface and introductory sections of the text. Most students, having overlooked those sections, missed the questions—thus forfeiting a grade of A. We learned, from this punitive experience, that all the sections of all the books were fair game.

As I have learned to teach, I too have been interested in my adult learners taking notice of and appreciating the entire text—all the sections. While I am not interested in posing obscure questions on tests, I am interested in students getting in touch with all that any book has to offer. Authors take quite seriously the writing of the sections that come before the principal content. For many writers, much time and great effort is spent in the pages that precede the content. Writers are hoping that the front matter invites the reader into their work.

From a publisher's perspective, books are generally divided into three sections: front matter, principal text, and back matter. The front matter is the material at the front of the book that usually offers information about the book, about the author, about the author's intent, and about the presumed audience. The front matter is not the principal text, but the "get ready" information for the principal text. The front matter is the author's opportunity to set the tone for the readers' experience. It offers a framing of the text.

Reading the front matter is like watching the beginning ten to twelve minutes of a film. In these opening scenes, the filmmaker is establishing the pretext of the storyline with images, sounds, pace, and rhythm to pique the viewers' interest. Or the front matter is like the moments of boarding a roller coaster ride. It is like when we are being harnessed in, then the thrill of the ever-so-slow trip up the steep incline. Creating anticipation of the ride is what the front matter is about.

In many of my courses, I would guide my students in lingering over the front matter. I wanted my students to have their appetites whetted. I wanted their anticipation to be heightened. During class sessions I would, with my students, review the provided front matter sections. I would rehearse all the sections: copyright page, dedication, epigraph, table of contents, foreword, preface, acknowledgments, introduction—any pre-sections that the author had provided.

Please know that as I am extolling the virtue of and necessity of front matter, I am not saying that the back matter should be overlooked or disregarded. The footnotes, endnotes, appendix, bibliography, and the index are important. My experience is that students, when needed, find their way to those tools provided in the back matter. It is the tools of the front matter that I think need support for our students' improved reading habits.

As I reviewed the front matter with students, I would make sure they knew how to decipher the codes of the copyright page (for many, this was their first experience knowing this code). I would call their attention to the dedication as it usually provided a personal and loving note from the author. We would read the epigraph and discuss whether the author was providing a summary or a counterexample, or was juxtaposing their work with a wider literary canon. I would ask, "To what is the author inviting the reader?"

I would point out that the typeset design of the table of contents is meant to communicate as much as the listing of the chapter titles. "Read the design as much as you read the words," I would say. We would read aloud the foreword, preface, and introduction, then invite the students to compare and contrast the three sections. I would remind them that the author has free range concerning the role, responsibility, and weight of each of these sections, and each author decides how these sections will function as preliminary for the reading of the text.

I would suggest that these sections tell us something important about how the author is thinking, and I would ask them to speculate or extrapolate what the author is promising. Sometimes, I would break the class into small groups to read and report back the role of each section or to report back a comparison of all sections. Finally, I would say, "We have saved the best for last!" The best way to understand the motivation of an author, the way to see into the author's soul, is to read the acknowledgments. Writing about an author's gratitude is to write about one's own heart. Acknowledgments provide glimpses into the writer's process, and likely, insight into the writer's project which, invariably, is bigger than the book at hand.

Some groups, by the end of the semester, began to ascertain that—for some authors—the promised book in the front matter was not the book in principal content. With these observations, I knew they had become better readers.

Once students develop better reading habits they become better learners, better thinkers, and more able to understand the complexities and curiosities of other people as well as their own people. I discovered that taking time to teach adult students good reading habits is time well spent—for me and for them.

FOR REFLECTION . . .

1. What better reading habits do you think your students need?
2. How do you help students develop better reading habits?
3. What practices described above would you find helpful?
4. How do you help students move from description, to response, to engaging with self and other ideas, to making critical use and judgments?

47

Hard Teaching Against Racism

Teaching for racial equality, and against oppression, has meant coming to grips with what my adult students (domestic and international) do not know, i.e., the basic concepts of race and the mechanisms of racism in the United States. Teaching about racial violence, domination, and societal hatreds invariably means asking students to relearn their views on race, as well as to become critically astute concerning issues of Western society and systemic oppression. Institutionalized white supremacy is a delicate and emotional subject.

Many students report that the conversations in seminary courses are their first critical, extended conversation about the "isms" (racism, sexism, classism, etc.). While I am not surprised, I am alarmed. I can but hope that their exposure to these conversations will compel them, in their own communities of responsibility, to lead more life-giving dialogues. If Black lives are ever to matter, we need religious leadership who understand the death-dealing institutions that frame our capitalist democracy and the targeted violence that ensues for the minoritized.

Extended conversations on racism and violence are embedded in my Introduction to Educational Ministries course. Among the students, the required course, with conversations on attitudes of white supremacy and class privilege, has the reputation of being HARD. I have done little to counter the hallway chatter because I think (re)learning race identity and the theory of racism is HARD work. It is not a soft, warm, and fuzzy dialogue. It does not build self-esteem or use the approach of "I'm OK / you're OK." It is a conversation that most people would rather avoid. It is a conversation where I push past triteness, trivialities, and pleasantries.

After teaching about racism for these many years, I have a list of concepts that students have told me, through their comments, silences, and behaviors, is the stuff that has caused the most cognitive dissonance. Rethinking what they thought they already knew is confounding (HARD). The biggest and most consistent surprise is that race is not a biological reality. Race is a social construct based upon cultural norms. Beyond this fact, they are also halted by the following:

- The traditions of race and racism in the United States have a history that needs to be studied. For example, at one point in US history, it was theorized that there were thirty-five white races.
- Laws and social practices create race based upon differences seen through the lenses of culture.
- Public policy by federal and state government (e.g., US Constitution, Emancipation Proclamation, Affirmative Action, Civil Rights Act, Voters Rights Act, etc.) has been the scaffolding of systemic racism, as well as anti-racist thought.
- Whiteness is not universally normative. The values, mores, and behaviors (e.g., beauty standards, gender roles, worldview concerning community) espoused by whiteness are not essentialist.
- Whiteness is one culture (albeit powerful) in the mosaic of global cultures.
- Whiteness is more than skin color or ethnic origin. It is about privilege and access to opportunities, power, and wealth acquisition reserved by public policy and private action for those deemed as white.
- Housing, wealth, education, and inheritance are systemically racialized by public policy. Differences are not deficiencies.
- Those of us who are different from white, e.g., African American, Latine, Asian, Native American, etc., do not have to compare ourselves to whiteness for legitimacy of culture or ontological presence.
- Non-white people are not inherently flawed; we are not divinely created as a holy mistake.
- Racial markers (like skin color, hair texture, shape of eyes or nose) are assigned cultural values. The body, then, is the site of violence/

de-humanization because it is believed that by viewing the body one can accurately identify race, and thus is instantly able to assess the power and worth of a person.

And perhaps the most insidious of all, students are surprised when they are told those who benefit the most from racism are oftentimes the least aware and critically articulate about the phenomena of racism. Those with white privilege are privy to the spoils of a racist system even if they are not personally racist. Keeping the oppressors unaware and inarticulate is a strategy of the successful, racist architecture. At some point during these uncomfortable conversations, I tell my students that I expect them, now armed with this knowledge as well as with an awakening curiosity, to change the world into a less hate-filled place. I assure them that to assist persons with the burden of white supremacy is dangerous work, but the work of justice in the twenty-first century demands it. Then—for relief (theirs and mine)—I play "Awake Up Everybody" by Harold Melvin & the Blue Notes.

FOR REFLECTION . . .

1. What would it mean to educate yourself and colleagues about the basic structures of racism in classrooms? Other than this essay, what resources might be read and discussed?
2. How could class topics, goals, selection of texts, classroom practices, assignments, and outcomes embody liberation and anti-racist principles?
3. Create a faculty culture that talks openly and honestly about racism and the ways it permeates the curriculum.

48

Letters of Gratitude

So central to my identity is teaching that when I think of the highest honor, the highest appreciation, I think of my gratitude for those who have liberated me through their teaching. I aspire, then, to instill in my students an appreciation for their dearest teachers. I want them to experience the practice of gratefulness as I believe it is a healing practice. When the cold, achy heart feels the warmth of gratitude—that warmth soothes, relaxes, and heals. I want my students to experience gratitude as that experience is a powerful spiritual salve for the wounded heart. Consequently, I have designed a learning activity that encourages the experience of gratefulness for teachers by students.

The assignment is straightforward and elegant. These are my instructions: (1) Recall a teacher who changed your life. The person might be a professional teacher who you encountered in grade 3 or graduate school. Or, equally acceptable, the person might be your grandmother, your scout leader, your friend. The recall might be focused upon a recent event, or it might focus upon a relationship from long ago. The relationship might have lasted for years and years, or the relationship might have been a week or two. Recall a person who taught you deeply and well. (2) Sit with this memory. Let the memory take full flower in your mind. Linger with the memory so that it is vivid. (3) Using the categories of liberation as described by Dr. Anne Streaty Wimberly in her book *Soul Stories: African American Christian Education*. Name, describe and reflect upon the ways your teacher liberated you. (4) As your analysis and reflection deepen and take shape, write a letter of gratitude, in first person, to your teacher articulating (in the theological and pedagogical language of our class) the liberation you experienced. Your letter of gratitude should be five to seven pages double-spaced, with citations from our readings and lectures.

Over the years, I have probably read no fewer than one thousand letters of gratitude written by my students to teachers. Each batch of letters feels like waves of love. Liberative teaching can be such a powerful change-agent in the lives of students that when students express their awareness and appreciation the written word becomes electric. The letters are love letters—healing for the heart for those with gratitude as well as those ingratiated.

A few years ago, I added a new dimension to the assignment. Out of all the letters I receive in any given class, I select a sampling of letters to be read aloud in class by the author of the letter. I want students to hear their own voices when in tones of gratitude. During the readings, fellow students hear the analysis of good teaching by peers, and the readings also infuse our classroom with the teeming, energetic vibration of gratitude and gratefulness.

Students will often cry as they read their letters. It is, I have been told, a revelation, to speak your deep gratefulness aloud in front of witnesses. The intimacy of liberation is revealed.

I encourage students to mail their love letters to their teachers. If the teacher has died, I encourage students to find a ritual way to honor the teacher—light a candle, grow still and quiet, read the letter aloud prayerfully as if your teacher is present . . . and wait.

Every now and then, a student will tell me that there has been no one in their lives for whom this kind of letter might be possible. They report that there is no teacher who is deserving of such gratitude or whose efforts warrant heartfelt gratefulness. I tell them to take more time in recollection. If they return still without focus—I tell them to take more time in recollection because without such a relationship I doubt if they can ever be a transformative teacher for someone else.

I know some students have written letters of fiction—letters to people who they wish had been in their lives. I am glad they found a way to get at the work, even in their own imaginations. This gives me hope. Only once have I had a student choose to submit no letter because there was no one to write to or imagine. I still pray for this man.

I invite all of us to write a long, thoughtful, heartfelt letter of gratitude to the teacher who liberated us (follow the directions above). Then, mail the letter.

FOR REFLECTION . . .

1. Be mindful that letter writing as a form of creative writing often encourages students to think in new and needed ways. What writing assignment might be converted to the format of letter writing to deepen student engagement?
2. Do the assignment. Write a letter of gratitude, in first person, to your teacher articulating (in the theological and pedagogical language of the class) the liberation you experienced.
3. Mail the letter.

PART FIVE

SCHOOLS—Communities of Colleagues

What does it mean to be a faculty colleague? What stake do I have in my institution? How do we build environments that nurture teachers and enhance learning? How do I honor and engage those who work with me? What do I do when I sense trouble in my school? Am I thriving here? What is my teaching life?

49

With a Little Help

THE WEEK AFTER GRADUATION, I got a call from a dear colleague. He was working on his syllabus for the upcoming summer semester. Having been in conversation for twenty years, he and I—like the Beatles' song—"get by with a little help" from each other. My colleague is a brilliant, multidisciplinary scholar. Unlike me, he reads deeply across several academic fields—both domestic as well as international literature. He brings that expansive knowledge to our collaboration. I bring to our collaboration my scholarly knowing and, more important, my know-how in creativity, imagination, and the ability to make unorthodox connections in pedagogy, cultural politics, and beyond.

Our phone conversation was as usual. My friend began by describing the focus of his upcoming summer course as well as the theory he was emphasizing in the course. He quickly summarized the required readings. He reminded me that it was a summer intensive, so he needed assistance in making good use of the time format. I asked if he needed to talk about assignments or learning activities. He said both. I took a few deep breaths, considered his topic, then intentionally imagined the graduate students in his course. Half of the enrolled students would be students of many races born in the United States, who will likely go on to serve religious communities close to home. The other half would be international, coming from countries in Asia, Africa, and the Caribbean, who might either serve white churches in the United States or return home after graduation. My friend waited patiently as I thought. After my long pause, I asked, "Are you ready?"

He said yes. I launched in by asking questions of clarification as if I were a student in his course.

During that part of our conversation, he could hear the gaps in the course objectives and learning outcomes, and he began to strategize ways to narrow the gaps and more directly address the students' likely curiosities. Then, I brainstormed out loud about possible classroom activities that could take him and students out into the community near the theological school. We talked about possible resource persons to be brought into the classroom to make vivid the need for praxis-thinkers and doers.

Once I got all my initial ideas spoken, I stopped. I asked if he wanted more.

He said yes, so I continued. Next, we turned to possible assignments as well as ways to elicit questions from students that would help them to bridge theory with community. By the end of our conversation, my friend had more than enough material to finish designing his summer intensive. The course was going to be brilliant!

Our conversation was so well choreographed because of our reciprocity. I assist him with course development, and he helps me with editing and thinking more deeply about my publications. He has read and commented on almost everything I have published. I strengthen his work, and he strengthens my work. We know our work is better because of the input of the other.

Beyond the necessity of collaboration to strengthen and deepen our work, I would suggest networking is an underutilized aspect of teaching and friendship. A little over a year ago, an alum from my school called me and asked if she could put me in touch with a friend of hers who was working on a new project. I said yes, only because of the respect I have for the former student. I was not, at that time, looking for any new projects nor was I looking for a consultant. Now, two years later, the person she put me in touch with, who is neither an educator nor a theologian, has become a consultant for our seminary, and we are doing innovative programming in new areas. Had the consultant "cold called" me, I would have brushed him off. When a person I knew and trusted asked me to give time for a conversation, it was because of her influence that I paid attention and opened doors. Making use of our networks is opening ourselves to possibilities beyond ourselves.

Making use of our networks entails that many of us must come to grips with the cachet and influence of our roles. So many of us undervalue our social position and make little use of the societal, intellectual, and material capital that we are afforded in our positions as teacher/scholars. We are people with juice! Making use of that juice for other people is part of our jobs.

A new friend, who I met a year ago, told me that she drives her son to New Haven each morning for school. Since the commute is almost an hour, she stays in New Haven and writes at a local coffee shop, then picks up her son from school and returns home in the late afternoon. She is a professional writer so writing in a coffee shop is okay. I frowned at the thought of her working daily in a public coffee shop. The next day I phoned a colleague at a school in Connecticut. I asked him to take my writer friend to lunch because I thought they would enjoy each other's company. I also asked him to give her whatever he could. I told my writer friend to expect a call from my professor friend and to accept the lunch invitation. They had lunch, and she now has access to the school's library where she works each day. He got a new and needed conversation partner for writing, editing, and publishing. All I did was recognize that I knew a guy who could help my friend, then I made the phone call.

A project I used to direct was sponsoring a week-long conference for spiritual writers about improving writing and getting published. We believed that public theology is, in part, about getting new voices into the marketplace. The week-long conference had several worship services built into the schedule. I called a friend and asked her to plan and lead the worship services. She agreed, but asked why I did not do them myself. I said, "Because you will do them better."

The participants at the conference marveled that, during worship, we focused contemplatively upon the lives and prophetic witness of Toni Morrison, Mary Oliver, and James Cone. My friend, by way of liturgy, juxtaposed the ancient prophet Habakkuk's text, which reads in 2:2, "And the LORD answered me: 'Write the vision; make it plain on tablets, so he may run who reads it,'" with the lives of the prophets Morrison, Oliver, and Cone. The final movement in every worship service was then to challenge the conference participants to align with these great persons in their own work of writing the vision. By the feedback and reports, the worship experiences for the aspiring faith writers had mystical, transformative qualities.

So much of scholarship is constructed upon the flimsy falsehood of individualism, isolation, and self-aggrandizement. We make a mistake when we keep our work and our wants in isolation—hiding our light under a bushel. Our fears of having our ideas stolen, or having people turn down a request, or of opening to the possibility of ridicule and shame must be overcome. Our work as scholar/teachers is best done in community, in conversation, with other people.

Yes, I could tell you of a few incidents when my ideas have been stolen or simply attributed to someone else. But these derisory experiences do not keep me from the joy and accomplishments that can only be realized through collaborating, networking, and using my cachet to facilitate the ideas and dreams of others in my community. My greatest successes have been due to the love, support, and generosity of people who have helped me elevate my work, rise to the challenges of certain projects, and seen greater possibility in me than I saw in myself. This is the payoff of collaboration, networking, and friendship. This is the marvel of being part of an intellectual community.

FOR REFLECTION . . .

1. Name two or three friends who you contact regarding your teaching and scholarship. What do you share with them? What do you ask of them? Describe the feelings, the challenges, and the support.
2. Think about two or three friends who contact you regarding their teaching and scholarship. What do they share with you? What do they ask from you? Describe the feelings, the challenges, and the support.
3. Now think about your institution. Is there a network that helps you thrive? Who is in that network? To whom do you turn for support and friendship?

50

Knowing the Storm

ALL STORMS ARE NOT the same. A light summer rain is not a category five hurricane. You must learn, in your context, to identify those storms that can be refreshing, and even enjoyable, and those storms that are life threatening and require you to batten down the hatches or evacuate.

My Uncle Frank was a loving and unconventional man. He stood about six feet four inches tall. He had a medium build. He was bald on the top of his head with a hair-ring around the sides. He wore a size fifteen shoe and an extra-large hat. Uncle Frank was light-hearted and laughed often. He and my parents had grown up together in Cleveland, Tennessee. The Meridiths, the Bullocks, and the Westfields had known each other for many generations. By the time my brother and I were born, Uncle Frank and Aunt Emma, with their four children, lived in Philadelphia—near our family. My father treated Uncle Frank with the respect given an older brother.

Our families were family to each other.

Uncle Frank worked for a company that would buy out the local amusement park for its employees the Sunday of each Memorial Day weekend. Frank would accept the five tickets given each employee, then barter, negotiate, and acquire twenty or thirty more tickets so he could host a grand picnic for the extended family. My birthday is May 28; we would celebrate at the amusement park. Every year Uncle Frank would tell me the picnic was for my birthday. I loved Uncle Frank and Uncle Frank loved me.

Uncle Frank would reserve a pavilion in the picnic section of the park just for his guests. The annual event felt like a family reunion. Upon arrival at the pavilion, each family would claim two or three picnic tables and set up their spot. Each family brought food and beverages, more than enough to share. The picnic was a grand feast with all-day rides, card playing (spades, bid whist, pinochle), lots of laughter, and being together. It was a day of excitement and fun.

I have fond recollections of all my amusement park picnics, but there was one that was the most remarkable.

It was a sunny Sunday. Our family arrived at the park about 10 a.m. We parked in the parking lot, then hauled our food and picnic supplies from the parking lot to the reserved pavilion. After greeting everyone, my brother, father, and I left my mom to set up our picnic tables. We went to ride the rides, promising to return in two hours for lunch. We started with a ride on the Wild Mouse—the wooden roller coaster. Then the bumper cars, Ferris wheel, and then the teacups. It happened when we were in line for a second ride on the roller coaster.

Without warning—the wind whipped up with prolonged gusts. The sky darkened. It began to drizzle. The drizzle turned into a downpour. My dad told us we needed to go back to the pavilion. My brother complained because he wanted to ride, even if it was raining. Dad grabbed my hand, told my brother to move quickly, and pointed in the direction of the pavilion. With a pout, my brother trotted ahead of us. The downpour increased. As we jogged, it seemed as if everyone in the park was running—looking for shelter from the storm. It was pandemonium.

By the time Dad, brother, and I got near to the pavilion the rain was teeming from the skies. The thick rain made it difficult to see. The winds were erratic. My mother was standing at the edge of the pavilion watching for us and, no doubt, praying. When Mom saw us at a distance, she began to call my father's name and wave her arms. Dad picked me up, grabbed my brother by the hand, and jetted to my mother. Everyone in the pavilion was packing up. My mom dried us off with an extra tablecloth and paper towels.

As if out of nowhere, Uncle Frank ran into the pavilion and hollered, "Don't leave!" Hearing Frank's voice, people paused. Everything but the rain and the wind stopped to listen. Frank said, "Don't go! The storm is not going to last long. Don't go!" Several families ignored him—packed quickly and launched out into the mean weather headed back to the parking lot to drive home. Uncle Frank came over to my parents and repeated, "The storm will not last long. We are safer here than on the road." My parents hesitated. They did not know what to do. Uncle Frank collapsed a card table, leaned it against a pavilion wall and instructed me and my brother to go under. We did. Frank covered the table with a tablecloth and made sure there were no exposed edges to be caught by the wind. Uncle Frank instructed us, "Stay there until we call you out!"

The storm lasted another thirty or forty minutes. They were long and frightening minutes. Then, as abruptly as the storm started—it stopped.

With the stillness, my brother and I peeked out from behind the table. My father said, "Come on out, it's over." We crawled out and I looked around the pavilion. The only folks who had stayed were Uncle Frank, Aunt Emma, their four kids, our family, the Conway family, and the Simmons family. Anything uncovered in the pavilion was soggy or drenched, but no one was hurt.

As if by magic, the thick, black clouds continued to part, and the blue sky returned. The sun shone bright again. The winds were gone. Together we cleaned up the pavilion and reestablished our picnic. Families had left covered dishes, coolers, and lawn chairs. Dad and Frank organized items they would return in coming days. My mom and Aunt Emma took inventory of the food and reset one large table of food and a beverage station for everyone. Mercifully, my birthday cake was unharmed. In about thirty minutes we heard the amusement park rides restarting.

And here's the best part—for the rest of the day there were no lines for any rides!

Since most of the people in the park had fled during the storm, those of us who had braved the storm were now free to ride any ride without having to wait in line.

That day, I rode the roller coaster twenty-seven times! That day I rode every ride in West Point Park!

That day was one of the best . . . ever!

Years later, I asked Uncle Frank how he knew we should stay at the pavilion during the storm. He said, "All storms aren't the same. Even bad storms aren't the same kind of bad. That storm came up so fast and unexpectedly, I knew it was going to move through just as quickly. I also knew driving in that kind of weather would have been more dangerous than hunkering down in that pavilion." With a wry smile, Uncle Frank continued, "And it was your birthday—we had not cut the cake!"

Friends, storms in our careers are like this. Ask yourself, which storms are simply part of the ecology of faculty life, and which storms are potentially life threatening or cataclysmic? Negotiating the processes of hire, tenure, renewed contract, and promotion is distinctly different from navigating in an institution that is restructuring or has filed for financial exigency. Learning to advise students, lead faculty committees, and find a suitable publisher can be challenging, but all are elements of the academic landscape. How do you come to know what is usual and what is dangerous? We all need an Uncle Frank who can tell us if we should hunker down or run!

Thank you, Uncle Frank.

FOR REFLECTION . . .

1. Several possible storms in the academy are listed above: negotiating, advising, committee leadership, publishing. List some of the storms you are facing or have faced.
2. Think about one or two of these. Why do you name it a storm? To whom did you turn for support? What strategies of engaging did you find or use?
3. How do you define the difference between the usual and the dangerous?
4. How do you know when to "hunker down or run"?

51

Sharing the Gold

WITH PEOPLE ALL AROUND the globe, my attention was captured by the Paris 2024 Olympics. I tuned into the TV coverage as often as I could. Watching world class athletes perform their craft is spellbinding. Athletes performing at the highest level, pushing toward new world records and new personal best, rising to the challenge of being the greatest—all fighting to be number one. Winning the gold! It is riveting.

Track and field is one of my favorites, and this year the Olympics delivered high drama. American high-jumper Shelby McEwen along with New Zealand's Hamish Kerr both cleared 2.36 meters. In these kinds of moments, the rules of the game allow for a tie. If agreed upon by the athletes, both are awarded the gold medal. If the opponents do not agree to call it a tie, the competition continues until there is a definitive winner—a gold medalist and a silver medalist. The moment was tense. The officials consulted with the athletes. Rather than preferring the tie, Shelby McEwen opted for a jump-off with Kerr. Shelby preferred to continue the competition in lieu of sharing the gold medal.

In the end, Kerr of New Zealand took the higher jump to clinch gold, following eleven straight misses from the two finalists. It was a devastating outcome for McEwen, who was left with silver. McEwen went home having clinched second place.

For me, McEwen's decision was one of life's ironies. When I heard that McEwen opted out of the shared gold medal and wanted the competition to continue, I thought YESSSS! and NOOOO! at the same time . . .

Yeah! That's right. Don't settle for second best! You got this! Fight on! There's no "sharing" on the Olympic podium! Get your medal! Buckle down, concentrate, and win! You've trained long and hard for this moment!

NOOOO! What are you doing? Take the gold medal! Gold is what you have been training for. It's what you have been competing for. You earned it! Take it! Share it! There's no shame in sharing victory! No need to continue the fight! You won . . . well, you and the other guy won, but that's good enough!

I can understand McEwen's decision, and while I respect his decision, it troubles me. My fear is that we have been taught that a shared victory is a lesser victory, a suspicious victory, a sullied victory.

Opting out of sharing a gold medal, and then losing the gold for silver, is not a story we are used to hearing, or the story we like to tell. The silver medal is not "really" a win, and we like winners. If this had been an old Hollywood movie, McEwen in the final, dramatic round would have taken the gold. The old Hollywood story of winning rather than sharing must be interrogated, contested, reconsidered, and rewritten.

Doctoral students and faculty are not athletes. But the arena of the academy is highly competitive. We are in rarified environments where, in many instances, competition is prized over cooperation. Our competition includes making arguments, defending arguments, critiquing arguments, and doing our utmost at winning arguments. We are trained to compete against one another for awards, jobs, grants, and book contracts. And now, with social media, we compete for TV appearances, influencer status, and royalty checks. The academic competition is not fisticuffs, but it can be as abrasive as any athletic bout. Many colleagues are drawn into the academic arena because of their warrior spirit and battle skills. Others had to adapt and hone for the fight. Others, unprepared and unable, have just been beat up. Those in the academy know a fight. Given the lesson of McEwen, can we learn when to share the win?

I have no disdain for the competitive spirit. I enjoy friendly competition, especially if the winner buys the beer after the game. What I disdain is the way winning at all costs eclipses the love for what we do. Our passions are more focused on winning than on the practice and art of achieving, creating, and building. Honing collaborative efforts for stronger communities, networks, and relationships is more needed than fighting for the individualized win. It is not enough to train scholars to compete. Learning the skills and challenges of partnerships, collaborations, coalition building, and the sharing of wins is the way we create the path into our own future. My fear is that in our unrelenting competitiveness we lose out on or squelch the most brilliant minds or miss out on the far-reaching achievements that only occur in collaboration.

FOR REFLECTION . . .

As we reshape our educational ecologies, the question of teaching for, and with, collaboration is a critical question.

1. In your scholarship, do you expect to win while others lose?
2. Do you aspire to be the one and only, the star, while seeing little value in partnerships, collaborations, and shared accomplishments?
3. Do you pit your doctoral students one against the other for scholarships, grades, and your time and attention?
4. In your school ecology, are faculty colleagues who "win" in their fields given higher salaries and additional goodies, while other colleagues are invisibled or ignored?
5. Are your course learning activities and assignments geared to teach competition or collaboration?
6. What will it take to shift our faculty cultures to environments that support and celebrate sharing and the variety of contributions?
7. When you compete in scholarship, to what values do you adhere? Is "win at any cost" one of your refrains?

52

Senior Scholar as Historian, Gatekeeper, Elder

THE RANK OF SENIOR SCHOLAR is the highest and most revered. The hierarchy of the academy creates senior scholars by assigning newly minted faculty with the status of junior scholar, then over several years through a process of review, tenure, and/or promotion, some colleagues reach the status of senior scholar. Promotion to senior scholar, as either associate professor or full professor, is perceived as a badge of worthiness and nobility. The academy requires professorial participants to either ascend or be jettisoned. In some schools, earning the status of senior professor means having fought, brawled, struggled, and won.

Senior scholar status is entitled to previously unavailable resources, and opportunities—goodies not afforded the junior scholars. Senior scholars are expected to have responsibilities and obligations that are not the onus of junior scholars. However, at some schools, there is not a clear demarcation between the obligations of junior or senior scholars—juniors are given duties and responsibilities like, or aligned with, those given to senior scholars. All this is to say, there is a great deal of variation between schools when one considers the culture, hospitality, duties, and obligations attributed to junior/senior scholar status. I am not suggesting that one model is superior to the others. I am suggesting that one needs to read the context and know which model is functioning in the school where they are employed.

Who teaches senior professors how to be good senior professors? How do senior professors get mentored into their duties, power, influence, obligation? Who shows senior scholars how to transition from the institutional patterns, habits, and behaviors of junior status? How does the institution assist senior scholars in becoming their most generative selves in this season of seniority? By what process are senior scholars given permission to wield their power for the best impact upon students, community, and the institution's future? What if most senior scholars operate as novices in the community structure? What if, without senior scholars who are mindful and present, the community cannot become healthy nor flourish to its potential?

As I think of my own vocational journey, I have not been privy to conversations about identity as a senior scholar. Without benefit of critical reflection for planning, and without imaginative reflection for doing, it has not been easy to know what to do, or how to be, or what to be about, as a full professor. I have never been part of a conversation that helped me parse, decide, live into, or imagine how the authority of the rank of senior scholar could be used, might be used, or should be used. When I was promoted to the rank of full professor, I was glad for the pay increase. Equally true was my lack of interest in the institutional loyalty that was so often inferred by some administrators.

I have learned to be a senior scholar by watching and engaging, that is, by trial and error. I have learned from the modeling of others only because I paid attention to those in this rank and wondered about their lives and professional decisions. In so doing, I have noticed three personas of senior faculty, or three modes of professionalism for the highest faculty rank: gatekeeper, historian, elder. I am sure there are other modes. For now, I want to describe these three.

SENIOR SCHOLAR AS GATEKEEPER

The gatekeeper recognizes the power and influence of the highest rank and intentionally wields that power in decision making opportunities that form and shape the institution and its future. In acknowledgment of the gatekeeper's authority, colleagues assign the gatekeeper as chair of the most central and significant committees. The gatekeeper is consulted on major institutional decisions by the highest administrators including the trustees. If this persona is considerate, gracious, humble, community minded, and collaborative, the colleague is contributing to an ethos of cooperation, deep listening, and shared care. The danger of this persona is when the person operates through power-mongering, tyrannical, opportunistic, mean-spirited, and bigoted decisions. Schools can be treacherous when these people attend to maintaining the oppressive status quo, which results in deepening the toxicity of the school's ecology.

SENIOR SCHOLAR AS HISTORIAN

This persona works as being the reminder, the memory keeper, or the historian. Having served on the faculty for a long period of time, the person has a long memory from years of experience and participation. When the new people, new programs, new projects, or curriculum changes are considered, the person playing the role of historian will recount the moments when, in the past, a similar attempt was considered or made. The voice of the historian is often used to hold the institution accountable to the mission, legacy, and tradition. The historian often holds dear those colleagues who are no longer employed by the institution or no longer members of the faculty by invoking their names at meetings or telling stories about "the good old days." This persona can be quite helpful as an institution plans and is able, with memories of the past, to press forward and adapt. The person can also hold the institution hostage to the past and to earlier decisions that are not adequate for unfamiliar futures.

SENIOR SCHOLAR AS ELDER

This person may or may not be elderly, per se. This person recognizes that they are no longer in the fray of accomplishing status and rank and makes use of this phase of professional life to regularly provide insight, wisdom, and assistance to others. This person uses their power and influence to build community, mentor others, and be personally creative. They create time to regularly sit with individuals and groups for wise counsel. The communal role of the elder is reinforced by the way members of the community respect them and treat them with kindness, deference, and regard. They are admired and respected.

Elder scholars will often take on the mantle of making "good trouble" so that the more vulnerable colleagues are not blamed or do not receive retaliation in difficult institutional battles. They can afford to risk, stick their necks out, knowing their status means that they will receive little reprisal.

I suspect I most admire the mode of elder because I come from a tradition that promotes, and depends upon, those at the highest ranks to reach back, reach down, reach out, and help. The Black church tradition has its gatekeepers and its historians. But we revere our elders. In my tradition, we defer to Big Mama, Mother of the Church, the Saints, the Teachers, and the Prayer Warriors.

I am working on my elder persona.

The toxic environment that plagues so many faculties is not lodged in the brick, mortar, and drywall of buildings. The toxicity permeates the relationships of the community. The lack of care, unfriendliness, bigotry, and acts of dehumanization reside in the ways people treat one another. Toxic environments—relational patterns of ugliness, shaming, blaming, ruthlessness, and deadly competition—might be inherited, but they are upheld and maintained by our choices of continued violent behaviors, lack of relational skills, and low emotional intelligence. Senior scholars, as gatekeepers, historians, and elders have the power and authority to shift and repair toxic environments in schools—if we would.

FOR REFLECTION . . .

Think about the senior scholars at your institution. Think about your place in that institution:

1. Where do you reside in the context?
2. To whom do you turn?
3. Who makes the situation toxic?
4. Who provides guidance?
5. To whom is authority given?
6. How do you negotiate the context?
7. Now, consider the questions you now need to address. Who will you turn to for assistance? Are there some steps you think you need to take? Are there some commitments you need to make or rethink?

53

Feeling at Home or Not

Higher education is a by-the-book, highly structured reality. From syllabus design (written for students as well as for administrators) to navigating the tenure-track process and promotion process; from classroom lesson planning to student assessments; as well as the preconceived, even contrived ways articles and books are selected for publication—those of us who teach in the academic world participate in a rigid reality.

For a scant few colleagues, this rigorous reality creates spaces for thriving and the production of new knowledge. It is the promise of this constructed reality. Dangerously, the same austere reality creates ease and opportunity for those who are harbingers of racism, sexism, classism, and heterosexism to have tremendous platforms of harm against colleagues and students of color. The strata of oppressive, hegemonic forces in the larger politic of US society are duplicated in the reality of higher education with too few opportunities for checks and balances of justice and equity. Subtle and blatant acts of dehumanization go unchallenged. Gestures of ignorance and insensitivity are commonplace. Those colleagues who routinely wield their biases, prejudices, ill wills, and ignorance toward people of color and non-white cultures are too often gatekeepers in this reality. Challenged to navigate this strange reality and stymied to negotiate with persons who would see us fail, there is little sanctuary for us unless we create it for ourselves.

While scholarship is my passion and joy, I never feel at home.

My experience of displacement/up-rootedness is neither unique nor rare. For African American women and other colleagues who are othered and systemically marginalized, the reality of education is designed so that we remain strangers, even in the familiarity of academic spaces. Our outsider status is galvanized by the white feminist patriarchs, also known as patriarchs-in-drag, who refuse to do critical reflection on relationships with othered women and people of color. Elisabeth Schüssler Fiorenza dubbed this experience of oppression in its many forms as kyriarchy.[1] While naming the experience does not alleviate the circumstance, it does make me feel oriented . . . known.

To never be at home is to contend with the accusations that we cannot do "classical" scholarship while at the same time reeling from the critique that our ethnic/cultural approaches are quaint, interesting . . . exotic. Our work and scholarship are othered along with our personhood. This constant confusion sends firm messages that we are not safe, not welcomed to be authentic or real. Amid this zero-sum experience of hostility, we are expected to be grateful for posts designed for occupation by white men. In this environment students quickly clue into those who are unwelcome and deemed to be without authority, making our classrooms spaces unnecessarily conflictual and contentious. We are not at home. I have often heard othered colleagues describe this reality as the experience of being erased. Surely, as those who are *imago Dei*, made in the image and likeness of God, we cannot be summarily negated.

I am not sure when I started this habit, but it helps me survive/cope. Each spring, after commencement, I bring a laundry basket to my campus office. I gather up those personal items that adorn my office. I pack up the family photos, artwork, cards, and gifts given by students and friends throughout that year. I pack up my coffee mug, teapot, and snacks in my desk. I balance my potted plants on the very top, so they do not get damaged or squished. With heaping laundry basket in hand, I move out of my office. Once at home with my laundry basket, I incorporate those items into the décor of my home. My office plants are nestled among the other plants in my living room, home office, and bedroom. The artwork and other items find a place on the shelves and in the bookcases. Then, in late summer, as the fall semester approaches, I make the decision to move back into my office—or not. If I move back in, I go around my house picking and choosing those art pieces that will adorn my campus office and assist my work in the coming year. I discuss with my plants and ask for volunteers to come to my campus office. Once back in my office, I carefully place the photos,

1. Schüssler Fiorenza, *But She Said*, 8–9.

paintings, sculptures, and plants. I move back in, only for the year. Knowing I will move out gives me strength and courage.

Each year, this ritual helps me navigate the death-dealing space that is the academy. It reminds me of my choice and my freedom. This ritual rekindles my own agency and intrinsic power. I move back in because of my own choice and not out of obligation, confinement, nor to stave off erasure by these institutions. Those political practices designed to divide and conquer, which are meant to keep us feeling unwelcomed, are weakened when I exercise this agency. Moving out of my office each spring lets me know I am free to leave the institutions that do not nurture me or my kind. Knowing I have a choice helps me keep my rage in check.

Moving into and out of my office reminds me that I am not homeless. The confusion, disarray, and disturbance that would reasonably result from being unwelcomed has little sting and warrants only momentary guile when I remember that our particularity is our gift to the world from the Divine. We are a people for whom this racist, sexist, homophobic, patriarchic academic world is a reality that requires the skills of ornery-ness and imaginative cunning—skills at which we are quite adept. The knowledge and belief that the love, sacrifice, and values of our ancestors and wisdomkin are steadfast provides hope.

FOR REFLECTION . . .

1. Think about the word "home." For a few minutes, engage the feeling of being "at home." Think about the spaces you are recalling, the people, the surroundings, the colors, the concerns, the joys, and the hopes. You may want to take a few notes to yourself.
2. Now think about the setting where you work and your work. Think about the spaces you are recalling, the people, the surroundings, the colors, the concerns, the joys, and the hopes. Again, you may want to take a few notes for yourself.
3. Compare your list. Of course, the school is not your home nor a home, yet where in your school do you feel connected and supported to thrive? Where do you feel out of sync, that you do not belong?
4. Think about how you want to respond to these feelings. Are there people, tasks, rituals that you need to engage? Write a plan of a couple steps you hope to take.

5. Are there ways you might make your students and new colleagues feel more at home? List the ways.

54

Open Carry Laws Include Schools

If I get shot in my classroom—I'm gonna be mad!

Yesterday, a friend told me her church and nursery school were having shooter-on-campus drills for the staff and children. I wondered when our school was going to do the same. Sometimes my colleagues and I joke about what we would do if an active shooter came into our building. We joke about ways to protect ourselves by fighting back or by fleeing. One colleague said not to plan to assist her in the event of an intruder because, given the opportunity, she would be the first one out of her office window. I made a mental note to see if I could climb out of my window. Thinking about myself climbing out of my basement window tickled me until I remembered it was a strategy to avoid getting shot.

The list of schools, churches, and public events that have become killing fields is growing. News reporters occasionally entreat viewers to stay sensitive to the victims of these tragic events. Interviewers of distraught family members work hard not to appear prosaic. While we do not want to mute our reactions to reports of gun violence, the numbness is difficult to prevent.

One of the nine people shot by the twenty-one-year-old white supremacist in the 2015 Charleston church massacre was the grandmother of an alumna. Grandma was at Bible study when she was savagely murdered. When my student and I get together for lunch, we still talk about the aftermath of the killing, and I help her grieve.

The amount of effort I have given to the teaching craft has not included ways of staying alive in the face of a gunman in my own classroom (most of the assailants are men). Heretofore, the challenge and un-safety have been in ideas. The danger of classrooms has been in coaxing fearful or belligerent students into new meaning-making strategies, or different ways of understanding old traditions. Now, the real danger of potential gun violence feels like domestic terrorism. I am afraid, I am unprepared, and I feel edgy in the familiar safety of my own classroom. The possibility of gunplay in my school looms thick yet wispy in the ethers. I struggle to make sense of this faint paranoia because I know it affects my teaching.

In my Teaching Teachers to Teach course, should I teach self-defense and strategies for emergency evacuations? Should I review with students the open-carry laws of the state and nation? Should course preparation include time at the gun range? Suppose classroom attire included Kevlar vests and running shoes? Could I shoot back at a student who was shooting at me?

The first time I saw someone shot I was nine years old. One school night, my dad and uncle were going to the post office to mail household bills. I gladly tagged along because I enjoyed being with them. Our routine was that once we arrived at the post office, I would be handed the bundle of envelopes, then I would leap out of the back seat of the green Pontiac, dash up the stairs, and deposit the letters into the outside mailbox for quick delivery to their addressed destinations. With my uncle driving, we rode with ease—the radio playing, my dad and uncle chatting, and me enjoying the view from the back seat. My uncle turned the corner onto a one-way street—we were about a block from the post office. Without warning, shots rang out!—"POP! POPPOP!"—I struggled to see out of the window because my uncle, with cat-like reflexes, had slammed on the brakes, shifted the car into reverse and, with foot flooring the accelerator, began backing out of the street—all in one gesture. Since this was before the days of seat belts, my child-body shifted wildly with the momentum of the car. Even so, I saw a group of teenage boys chasing a lone boy who was limping as he ran. The limping boy ran across the street and up on the sidewalk, and then collapsed. A boy who was chasing him had a gun at the end of his outstretched arm. That boy ran over to the collapsed boy and pistol-whipped him as he lay on the sidewalk. As if the scene had been choreographed by Alvin Ailey, they all ran off down the dark street, into the night, as if on cue—all but the collapsed boy who lay bleeding and dead on the sidewalk. My uncle's skillful driving sped our car backward around the corner and away from the mayhem. Uncle commanded the car out into the intersection, then gunned the gas, propelling us forward into streets with no shooting teens. I stared from the back seat in horror.

My beloved friend Zenobia is a retired warden from New York City corrections department. She spent twenty plus years on Rikers Island and other prisons. Years ago, she used to talk with me about ways of assessing a room for my best escape in the event of emergency like a gun being fired in the room. When we sat in restaurants, she would casually ask me over her menu to tell her where the exits in the room were. I was to have noticed them and made mental notes as we walked into the space. Most days I could not answer the question because I had failed to take notice. I did not like this game. I resisted her teaching because I deemed those skills as needed only in places like prison. The applicability of Zenobia's lessons for my classroom setting is soul withering. Tomorrow, I'm gonna call her and ask for a refresher lesson.

I do not own a gun because if I did, I would undoubtedly use it. I would use it when I felt fearful or angry.

I do not think clearly when I am fearful or angry.

FOR REFLECTION . . .

An epidemic of school shootings has permeated our society. School leaders and public leaders are wondering how they can respond.

1. What are the policies and procedures at your school for an active shooter on school grounds?
2. How do you address mental health crises and difficult personal situations in a class?
3. Are there changes you need to request? Are there questions you and others need to address? Are there directions you need to recommend to administrators, deans, deans of students, the public?

55

Fear Will Make You Hurt Yourself

Fear is the anxiety that you are about to lose something you love, need, have rightfully earned, or deserve. Fear will make you hurt yourself, silence yourself, edit yourself in ways that contradict or disavow your own best pursuits. Since we teach who we are, showing up afraid will only serve to distort your teaching, raise the apprehension in your classroom, and model a sense of distrust. While I understand the impulse to be afraid, we must choose to live unafraid, especially in our own classrooms.

Uncertainty has been weaponized. Random acts of callousness have been normalized. Scarcity is being orchestrated. Universities are being pressured in strange and unpredictable ways. The enterprises of education are being guillotined. If there was ever a time that provoked fear, anger, and confusion for those of us employed in higher education—now is that moment. Even so, my hunch is that it is shortsighted to expect that preemptive acts will rescue anyone from the strategies of demolition and anarchy. It is not likely that the fight can be avoided—particularly for those trying to skirt it. While cowering from the fight is an option, we would be foolish to think that cowering from the attack will lessen the challenge. Fear will drive you to attempt ineffective strategies.

The other day a colleague emailed the Wabash Center asking that we remove their syllabi from our online collection. They were afraid the contents of their courses would be read as diversity, equity, and inclusion materials and did not want, given the political climate, to risk being castigated. I can understand their desire to avoid worry, but removing syllabi from the internet, at best, is misguided. The fact of the matter is that nothing is ever actually removed. Why would the colleague think that hiding materials would make them safe? In this climate, compliance has not been met with a cease fire. I recognize that the fearful colleague is following suit with many prestigious universities who have performed an audit of their own websites, purged language of welcome and belonging, then re-languaged their program descriptions for public consumption. I suspect our safety will depend upon the capacities of our intellectual leaders to decide not to be intimidated. Harvard is leading the way.

Today, a colleague teaching at a state university reported that their department chair announced that she had recommended to the provost a 60 percent cut in the department's budget. The department chair stated that she hoped that by volunteering the massive budget cut she would avoid the impending budget fights. Once colleagues were clear that this recommendation was made to preempt the department head from having to fight for their department's budget, the startle of colleagues shifted to rage. They felt betrayed. When the faculty pressed the department head for a rationale, the department chair explained that because they were close to retirement they were entitled to choose "peace" and avoid the impending, university-wide budgetary conflicts. Now, the department is waiting in fear. They are afraid that the department head's wanton actions communicated to the university the lack of importance of the entire department. Wittingly or unwittingly, the timid department head chose to conspire in her own demise. She had not considered the welfare of the community over her own fear-driven impulse to preemptively concede—or maybe she had. Evil takes advantage of self-absorption and is intensified.

We do not have the luxury of being afraid if it allows avoidance, silence, or being untrue to our central aims. Values that are easily discarded to avoid a fight might need to be reassessed, but now that crisis is upon us, conceding seems reckless. Safety is not ensured. We must know where we stand before the fight comes.

If we are doing our jobs of good teaching, teaching religion and theology inherently cultivates voiced students who critically and imaginatively critique the status quo. We know there are no dangerous thoughts; to those who would squelch wonder, imagination and freedom thinking itself is dangerous. If in this moment we waffle on this rudimentary aim of teaching—why did we choose teaching in the first place? And why do we remain in higher education classrooms? Certainly, the individual and collective answers to these questions will matter as we decide our engagement in the vitriolic challenges of this moment. May our fear not become our hallmark. The worst thing we can do is panic and allow our fears to be the guiding force.

FOR REFLECTION . . .

1. What do you do when you do not know what to do and you are afraid to do anything?
2. What habits and practices (sacred or otherwise) will calm you during extended crises?
3. Who is your wise counsel in the season of doubt and distrust?
4. How do you work through experiences of unprovoked or unforeseen change?
5. What if the challenge is bigger than your capacity to lead, to teach, to serve?

56

Calm and Routine Might Be a Sign of Impending Conflict

WHAT IS HAPPENING IN the world is happening to each of us.

On May 3, 2023, Dr. Vivek Murthy, US surgeon general, released an advisory calling attention to the public health crisis[1] of loneliness, isolation, and lack of connection between people in our country. Disconnection fundamentally affects mental, physical, emotional, spiritual, and intellectual health. Even before the COVID-19 quarantine, approximately half of the US adults reported experiencing measurable levels of loneliness and isolation. Since the quarantine, we can imagine the sharp increase in isolation and fear. We, students/faculty/administrators, are part of this affected demographic.

Newspapers, in small towns and major cities, provided news that fed democracy and linked people overwhelmed by otherness and isolation. In the recent past, print and digital news provided a "watchdog" service aimed at holding our civic institutions accountable. The newspaper industry has reported a period of immense disruption and financial distress leaving news deserts across the country. Public service journalism that spotlighted the major issues confronting communities has shrunk. This leaves residents without the information they need to discuss and to solve their problems. Whether delivered over the internet, airwaves, or in print, the lack of vitality in local news coverage exacerbates our feelings of isolation.

1. Murthy, *Our Epidemic.*

Our loneliness is further compounded by the dichotomized assumptions promoted through social media. People depend upon memes, sound bites, and social media threads for facts, storylines, and information on complicated issues. Students/faculty/administrators, like the public, are immersed in social media culture. The rhetoric of "us versus them" has saturated our thinking and has become a presumed framework of discourse.

The barrage of loss, hatreds, separation, grief, and rhetoric of division is affecting us—all of us.

We are living in an extended and deepening national moment of blaming, clenched fists, gritted teeth, and suspicion for people beyond our chosen tribes, beyond our chosen communities, beyond those people with whom we agree and have chosen political affinity. There is growing suspicion of difference. There is a feeling that "the other shoe is about to drop," without knowing when or what the shoe will be.

Here is the strangeness. While the country becomes more polarized and less informed—our daily lives and routines are relatively unchanged. How can it be—business as usual?

Our everydayness continues relatively unscathed. We shop in the same grocery store. Go to the same big box stores. Perform the activities of employment. Participate in the same schools, churches, and mosques. Use the same online streaming services.

While we suffer from profound loneliness, our everydayness has not changed much.

We are simultaneously uninterrupted and fractured.

Division and social upheaval are smoldering while we operate in the relative customary school year start. School has begun. Teachers/students/administrators are reconvening with the same rituals, rites, and routines as always. Syllabi have been distributed. Lessons have begun. Committee meetings are back in swing. At a glance, we look fine. Yet, fear and uncertainty are palpable.

We must be aware that loneliness, fear, and isolation tend to manifest, not where they are easily seen in our daily activities, but in our interior spaces. Our fears are performed in relationships. Our isolation becomes apparent when we are with one another. Our trouble, pain, and turmoil are witnessed when we are working together and with others.

The start of school makes us vulnerable to seeing and being seen. We are, when we gather back, reconstituting our relationships while we are knee deep in our loneliness. Our relationships expose our fears, isolation, and mental unwellness. Conflicts will soon arise. My caution is that, given the effects of the wider political climate, the veneer of calm and routine will soon dissipate. Are your classrooms ready for conflict?

The most vulnerable people are those who bring diversity and difference into the faculty/student body/administration. For those faculties and student bodies who have, recently or over a very long period, accepted the challenge of diversity—this is potentially a very troubled moment for teaching. Diversity (race, class, political, gender, nationality, creed) is precisely what is not tolerated in the growing US climate, and yet diversity is what is needed to move us away from isolation and toward conversation, toward peace, toward community.

The lack of tangible conflict, or the absence of specific dispute, does not mean that institutional fissures are not forming along the lines of diversity. Unaltered routines, unexamined practices, and undiscerning leadership will miss the hushed emerging crisis in community. Do not wait until difference turns into intolerance, vindictiveness, expressions of hatred, and war to invite your school into meaningful conversations.

There are no recipes, formulas, or road maps for this brittle moment. Your school must engage its own communities as they are unique in the world and as you live together in this uncharted malaise.

Gladly, there are some big ideas to which we can attend to help us make sense of the places where you teach and learn. Now, during the beginning of the semester, I find ways to collectively reflect upon these kinds of questions in anticipation of conflict:

- What are the consequences of difference? What are the effects of difference?
- What meaningful project can we work on together? What sustains us through conflict?
- What is a good conflict and how are disputes processed with fairness, with justice, and for maturity of community?

Consider facilitating these kinds of habits and practices in your school or in your classroom:

- acknowledge the diversity and celebrate it;
- make the community aware of the diversities that exist;
- demonstrate how diversity strengthens the mission of community;

- attend to creating cultures of respect and regard for difference;
- create conversation groups across diversity to listen to one another;
- construct institutional processes and protocols before there is conflict;
- create an ombuds position;
- message into the community that difference is a strength and not a weakness;
- design new rituals and rites that support and honor diversity;
- facilitate conversations on the nature of hatred and the detriment of animosity;
- create policies of zero tolerance for hate speech;
- work on practices of solidarity;
- make a communal project of peace, empathy, compassion, and forgiveness;
- admire courage and bravery;
- award truth telling;
- create artwork and expressions that honor difference;
- complexify dichotomous thinking;
- find ways for people to work together against divisiveness, objectification, and authoritarian assumptions.

When, not if, the ugly expressions of hatred and entitlement bubble up in your community—be ready. You will not have the luxury of feigning surprise. Conflicts, subtle or violent, will arise along identity fault lines, and your institution must be ready so that those targeted by the dispute are not severely hurt, ostracized, or killed.

FOR REFLECTION . . .

1. Explore the questions above with other colleagues and friends.
2. Note the strategies you use to thrive.
3. Note which of the practices above you want to facilitate in your classroom.

4. What other practices do you use or draw on? We all have favorite ones. Note them. What are their strengths and weaknesses? What should be added or attempted?

57

When the Problem Is Where You Live

Like many colleagues, a great joy of teaching is mentoring students into employment. I was well mentored, and I hope I have done well by my students. Recently, I received a call from a former student who has been serving in the local church and now wants to turn their attention to joining a faculty. While enrolled in graduate school, I knew them as a creative, capable, and dynamic student. I was delighted when they wanted to talk about the prospects of joining a faculty. During our conversation, they asked all the right questions and were well prepared, having studied the school to which they were going to send their application. I knew the school and I thought they would make a good fit with the faculty.

But as we talked, I developed reservations. I realized that the school was in the middle of the country and in a rural section of the state. I asked my former student if they had considered what it would be like to live in such a different culture and be surrounded by such different political climate than the one they had known for the last ten years. With some hesitation, they said that they did not think the location of the school mattered if the position was a tenure-track job in their field.

Ugh!

There is more to a successful career than the right job. What of the quality of life afforded to you by the geographic location of the school? Yes, learning to flourish on a faculty requires attending to the professional aspects of scholarship. Equally, or in some cases more importantly, flourishing also requires attending to the personal and familial aspects of life.

Where you reside, where you call home, where you locate yourself and your family is critically important to your teaching and teaching life.

Location matters.

BIPOC colleagues have a particular challenge when trying to live in rural areas, in middle America, or in predominantly white spaces where the police and the neighbors assume you do not belong in those neighborhoods simply by profiling your raced and ethnic body. What do you do when the quality of life within commuting distance of the school is inadequate—inadequate for the needs of your family, or even dangerous?

Racial ethnic colleagues struggle with:

- finding hair salons, barbershops, hair products;
- body care, medical care;
- locating foods of their ethnic preference or religious need;
- romantic options for socializing;
- making friends from similar culture or backgrounds;
- adequately prepared schools for children;
- jobs for spouses;
- religious temples and churches;
- gyms and recreational spaces that feel welcoming;
- holy day and holiday celebrations.

Yes—we can always drive an hour or more for these services and products. But the critical question is—what is the toll upon us and our families when our job location means that we must live in hostile towns, hostile neighborhoods, or spaces that are not attuned to our cultural identities and needs?

Issues of cultural compatibility, if not thought through, are potentially detrimental to a teaching career.

Consider . . .

Colleagues who are single or whose families have not relocated are especially vulnerable to feelings of isolation and loneliness. Trying to find community in spaces in which race and cultural identity are in the minority is especially challenging when living alone or apart from family and established relationships.

Colleagues have reported that their children attend schools as "the one and only" of the student body. Children feel isolated, exoticized, bullied, and alone.

Colleagues have reported insufficient medical knowledge and medical care for ethnic specific ailments.

Colleagues have reported being afraid when people in the grocery store or hardware store ask, "Where are you from?" or "Why are you here?" The clear message is that you do not belong here. The message is that the stranger in the community is deemed as being strange.

Colleagues have reported being afraid to vote during elections for fear that they will be targeted for violence since their vote will not align with the popular vote in that town, county, or region.

Colleagues have reported receiving support from school administrators when abused by a local police officer. We are glad for the support from the school, but what does it mean for this colleague to continue to live in a place of fear—where the police are known to violate civil liberties of Black and brown bodies?

In some cases, the locations are familiar enough, and navigable enough, to sustain a modicum of wellness as you work a job at the school. But living in years of being uncomfortable and feeling alone can take a toll. It has a price.

What is at stake if you live in environments that you experience as being harsh, unwelcoming, harmful, or isolating?

I have heard of three kinds of approaches to engaging this complex problem of location:

- Plan for the place where you are uncomfortable to be only temporary; plan to remain in the location for only a short amount of time; plan for the next position where you are more comfortable and know that your discomfort is only for a limited amount of time.
- Develop a new imagination for culture; learn to accept the culture of the new location; find pockets of friends, allies. Learn the nuances of the town and neighborhood and adapt for the long haul.
- Commute—be in the space as little as possible through a hybrid schedule; commuting, digital workspace and flexibility might be a key to survivability. Negotiate at hire to work from home when home is a space of compatibility and safety.

In all cases, home must be a sanctuary adequate to sustain your teaching and teaching life.

By the end of the conversation with my student, I had persuaded them that investigating the town and imagining how they would live there is as important as preparing for the job. I am supporting my student through the interview process. Should they be invited to join the faculty, they will be ready with a strategy of ways to make that place their home.

FOR REFLECTION . . .

1. Think about your current context. How does it help you thrive?
2. What are the struggles you face over and over?
3. What are the strategies you have used to address these struggles?
4. How do you draw on resources that help you thrive?
5. Name a strategy of finding "sanctuary adequate to sustain your teaching and teaching life" that you use.
6. Think of another strategy you should try.

58

Twenty-One Ways to Welcome BIPOC Faculty

It is well substantiated that the retention rate in predominantly white institutions (PWI) for BIPOC faculty is abysmally low. Newly hired BIPOC faculty in PWIs report feeling ignored, unwelcomed, even shunned by colleagues and students. They are treated as if, though hired for the job, they do not belong. Yes, there are some PWIs in which providing hospitality to BIPOC faculty is done well. However, the majority of BIPOC colleagues who leave employment after less than three years report that their reason for leaving hinges upon experiences of being treated inhospitably. With this assertion, I am not focused on overt acts of racism or discrimination. I am, instead, focused upon acts of cultural insensitivity, lack of basic social skills, and the inability of an institution to be caring, compassionate, and friendly to newcomers who are BIPOC.

What goes wrong? Simply put, the new people are not on-boarded, not offered kindness and warmth.

Climates of care, hospitality, and belonging do not just happen. An ethos of welcoming new people must be attended to by many, many persons. The habits and practices of care, compassion, and belonging when BIPOC persons enter the PWI must be painstakingly exercised and attended to conscientiously.

Regrettably, so many schools do NOT have systems for on-boarding, orienting, and providing for the arrival of new persons in the first six to nine months of employment. People feel unwelcomed because no one, in a robust and institutionalized way, is welcoming them.

I would like to offer this list of activities, rituals, and happenings for your context so that, from the very beginning, BIPOC colleagues feel a strengthening of ties and a genuine forming of connections. All these possibilities will not be for every context and every hire. Find what works for you and the person who is newly hired. Consider this list and, given your context, create new ideas of care for newly hired BIPOC colleagues:

1. Invite the colleague to meals hosted in their honor. These are not meant as informal committee meetings, but gatherings to get acquainted with one another. Decide if the meals are better in an area restaurant or hosted in a private home. In either case, ask about the person's dietary preference and restrictions. Who on your faculty gives the best parties? Soon after arrival, ask the best host to throw a party for the new BIPOC faculty and have fun.
2. If you are a well-established member of the community, do not be stand-offish. Do not hold up waiting for the new faculty to ask you to coffee. Take the initiative—invite the new person to coffee or a meal—with no other agenda than getting acquainted. During the conversation, listen more than you talk.
3. Develop a ritual of welcoming professors by having the president, provost, dean, or department head introduce the new colleague to their first class, then applaud wildly in front of students. Send the message to students that this new person is not on probation, is not still being interviewed, is not less significant as a faculty colleague due to race. Send the message that there is an expectation that all respect will be given to this colleague.
4. Invite the new person to participate in campus rites, rituals, religious services in a role of their own choosing.
5. Assist the person with finding a religious community for themselves and their family should they desire it.
6. Invite the person to the trustee meeting, alum gathering, student event. Plan to introduce and celebrate the arrival of the colleague at the event.
7. Invite the person to attend the campus sports event and sit in the location of honor.
8. Invite the person to the faculty retreat and make sure they have transportation to the location. If the venue is in a rural location where the

BIPOC colleague would be unwelcomed, or in danger, change the venue.

9. Make sure the person has club or institutional memberships that are common and available in that context. For example, membership to the local country club, membership to the local gym, membership to the local library, etc.
10. Connect the person to known childcare networks, if desired.
11. Inform the person of access to certain "insider" goodies, e.g., campus guest housing, coupons for travel, use of vacation properties, meals in the refectory, bookstore discounts, etc.
12. Connect the person with one or two colleagues (one from faculty and one from staff) who will take responsibility for on-boarding.
13. Assign an elder faculty colleague to mentor the person on issues of tenure, promotion, and institutional culture.
14. Make sure the person has necessary keys, identifications, computer accesses.
15. Help the person with office setup.
16. Make sure all available institutional documents are provided, e.g., employee handbook, campus calendar, trustee meeting minutes, faculty meeting minutes, organizational chart, phone and email directory, etc.
17. Connect the person with persons who have a similar family structure (persons caring for children, elderly, pets, etc.).
18. Help the person locate doctors, groceries, barber shops, hair and nail salons that are culturally woke.
19. Consider what is unique about the town, city, or area and invite the new person to participate in that regionally cultural event.
20. Create an "ambassadors" list, i.e., a profile of families who would welcome getting calls from new persons about issues as they arise.
21. Ask the new person what they need, or what their family might need, to secure a good quality of life in the new location, then work to provide for that need.

In the most hospitable schools, it is understood that all persons in the community have a role and responsibility in welcoming the new colleague—ALL PEOPLE—EVERYBODY! The key is for the new BIPOC faculty person not to feel alone, isolated, abandoned, unwanted, or suspect. In the words of my mother, Nancy B. Westfield, "You do not have to become friends with all the new people, but you do have to be friendly."

FOR REFLECTION . . .

1. Look at the list. Is there anything you would add?
2. Which strategies have you used to help others thrive?
3. What strategies will you begin to practice?

PART SIX

NEXT STEPS—Improving Imagination, Rebuilding, and Creating Anew

Where do I find strength, hope, and meaning? Am I living a connected, fulfilled, and embodied life? Am I thriving? What is next—How do I live into the future?

59

Running Wild

Creative teachers are sometimes labeled as people who run wild—meaning we are people whose boundaries are too wide, whose disciplinary habits and practices are too flimsy, whose appetites look beyond what is safely seen, commonly known, or conventionally acceptable. I am a creative who has, for many years, made a practice of fostering wildness in my classrooms.

I believe that the invitation of teaching is for students to join in with running wild, i.e., create new worlds, grapple with unsolvable problems, cross boundaries as a gesture of connection and justice seeking, build stairways as we climb to uncharted heights. I have met many colleagues who concur with the aspiration of running wild! but who are too afraid, too anxious, too self-conscious, too hobbled to risk shaping classrooms from this vision. Teachers fear that if they move from a content driven classroom to a classroom that is learner centered, then the students will run wild over the teachers! The fear is that the wildness will make a shambles of the intellectual endeavor, embarrass the teacher, and shame the institution. This fear can be tamed.

Before joining a seminary faculty, I worked for many years as the minister of Christian education at a NYC church. I revamped their large Sunday school. In this seven-year process, I learned about teachers' eagerness to teach freely, with creativity and openness and the ways that that eagerness can be snuffed out by fear of losing control of the classroom.

Before the start of our fall classes, the church school teachers participated in three weekends of teacher-training using a laboratory method.

During this training, we rehearsed the curriculum through practice sessions. This allowed us to get acquainted with one another, do lesson planning, develop new skills, and have fun. We learned to teach by teaching.

At the first teacher meeting of the fall, I gathered the teachers to discuss their work and to reflect on the first three Sundays of teaching. After having observed their teaching for the first three Sundays, I had an overall negative criticism of their teaching. I was nervous about giving this feedback. I was anxious about their reaction. I decided to be straightforward. The eighteen of us were seated together at the table. I spoke in a warm but firm tone. I said,

> When I walk the halls listening to your classes, I mostly hear your voices. This means that, primarily, you are learning the materials you are teaching by rehearsing the lesson—out loud to the students. Remember our teacher training sessions? We do not want classrooms filled with your voice. We practiced activities that invite the students into energetic lessons.
>
> (I paused in hopes they would remember the training and practice.)
>
> I want to hear the voices of the students. I want to hear the children's voices engaging the lesson with their questions, concerns, laughter, reading aloud, talking to you and one another. When the children are the primary speakers and doers in the classroom, they are more likely to learn, retain, and be engaged with the lesson.

I felt the nervousness in the group rise. Two teachers pushed their chairs back from the table. One teacher folded his arms across his chest. The fifth grade teacher spoke up:

> Lynne, I need to be honest. You give us creative activities to do with the children, but I am afraid of losing control of the classroom if I let the children do too much talking or move around the room too much. If I do the talking, I am in control. I'm afraid they will run wild!

I threw up my arms like someone had made a touchdown and shouted,

> YESSS! Thank you! You are exactly right! Thank you for your honesty and good observations. Thank you for disclosing your fear.

This playfulness lowered some of the tension in the room. The tenth grade teacher still sat with his arms folded across his chest, and now a scowl on his face.

I continued,

> You are right. We do not want chaos in the classrooms with children running amuck. Nobody learns when students are out of control. But we know that students learn best when they are the ones engaged in activity. The various learning activities allow them to take hold of the stories and learn by participating. Sitting quietly teaches them to sit quietly, and that Sunday school is an uninteresting and voiceless place. We want children to learn by doing, interacting, questioning, exploring, investigating, wondering, and playing. And I need you to teach in these ways.

I paused for pushback. But no pushback came. I continued,

> Please, try some of the more creative activity options in the curriculum. I assure you that chaos will not ensue. The children will have fun and so will you.

The fears articulated by the Sunday school teachers are the same kinds of fears I hear from colleagues about their adult students in college, university, and seminary settings. That is, teachers fear that if they loosen their grip on a session that the students will say or do something Wild! Something unanticipated, unwanted, unhelpful, unplanned that will embarrass the teacher or show the lack of a teacher. Teachers fear that loosening control will put them in danger of being exposed as frauds or imposters. These fears are real. Sometimes these fears are paralyzing or debilitating. These fears can be calmed and overcome.

Teaching, with practice, can be improved if you are willing to give up control. For many professors, this teaching tactic feels counterintuitive and too risky, but my experience knows it to be true.

If we surrender content driven approaches—then what will happen?

I am pleased to report that none of the Sunday school teachers stormed out of the meeting that day. Each teacher, in their own way, slowly over the years of their commitment, learned to select the learning activities that involved arts, crafts, a wide assortment of storytelling methods, and even trips to other parts of the building. I noticed that the primary motivation for their risk taking was the feedback they received from their students.

When the learners were invited to become the storytellers replete with costumes, paints, and instruments, their glee was palpable. Enthusiasm grew when the students knew the lessons could include map making, puppet designing, interviews with pastors, or baking the communion bread. Excited children began arriving at Sunday school before the start time and asking to stay after the end time. Teachers moved from being reticent to feeling confident when they discovered learners were not there to judge their efforts but were there to benefit from their teaching.

Over the seven years, we moved away from being a place of instruction and toward becoming a community of learning—the teachers were the agents of that wild move!

FOR REFLECTION . . .

1. What are your creative or artistic interests, and how might you bring those interests into your classroom's learning activities?
2. What amount of time do you need for course preparation when planning for learning activities that are multidimensional and creative?
3. What funding is available for supplies, resources, excursions, and exhibits?
4. Who can you partner with to create a more vibrant experience for your students?
5. Note the phase "running wild." Name a time you indeed ran wild in your teaching.

60

World and Classroom

A LONG-STANDING APPROACH TO education meant that the student would sequester from the world, study undisturbed from the goings on of the world, to then emerge and return to the world as a learned person. The time away from society, family, and many kinds of communal obligations was meant to provide time for intellectual maturation, contemplation, and, some say, an extended adolescence. The students would be free to read, write, and think while under the watchful eye of a teacher. In the cloistered model of education, the degree taken (wrestled and snatched) afforded the recipient a select spot in the ranks of the higher echelons of society.

The focus of education as secluded and separate from society is evident in the language of students. Students talk about the classroom as being "in here" while their lives are "out there." Students, in rebuffing some ideas, comment "that won't work in the real world" or "that's nice to discuss, but in the real world people will not go for that." The classroom, for these students, is not the real, while life in society, in community, with family obligations and responsibilities is the real. Students also signal that what is taught in many classrooms has little relevance to the problems and pain of their people. Or what they learn requires a great deal of translation, interpretation, and adaptation to be relevant to the suffering of their people. The primary aim of cloistered teaching is to insulate student and teacher until which time the student has met the disconnected standards of the faculty.

Yet is this "sequestered view" of learning really what occurs? Our lives, our stories, and our realities all intersect with our learning. In times of shifting models of education, these kinds of new questions abound:

- Suppose the aim of education is not to hide from the world to emerge as an educated person, but instead the better aim is to prepare to meet the needs of the world as education?
- Could this moment be forcing us to a collective realization that the better aim of education is to engage in the world as education and thus change the world?
- What is the relationship between communities of learning and social change?
- What is and should be the influence of the world upon classroom teaching?
- Moving forward, what will be the relationship between communities of learning and the world?
- What will be the relationship between schools and the very neighborhoods, towns, and cities they occupy?
- What if the world is the classroom?
- What practices of communities of learning are needed for social innovation?
- What meaning-making practices, understandings, and joys of the world are needed to facilitate vibrant learning in schools?

Yes, many schools have forms of internships, field education, supervised vocational experiences, elaborate field trips, or study abroad while in a degree program. Most of these programs are auxiliary to the degree program, and if not auxiliary the experiences that keep students in the world or send students into new worlds are not the spine of the curriculum. The primary presumption of current models of higher education is that students first learn theory in a classroom (cloistered), then are sent out into the workplace to practice. There is still a separation and privileging of theory over practice. Howard Thurman informed us years ago that theory and practice are each sides of the same coin. What would it mean to create approaches to education that do not separate theory from practice or student from community?

A small start to answering this critical question has to do with the mindset of the students while in a degree program. The identities and social locations of my students have always been a significant factor in my teaching. I wanted my students to come to class and bring with them conversations about the joys, suffering, trouble, practices, learnings, and know-hows of their people, their communities. I believe that students, to have agency in their own learning, must not leave their families or society for education, but they must reflect critically and imaginatively on the struggles of their community, looking for new and needed solutions. To facilitate this approach, I designed this learning exercise for my introductory course:

During the second session of the course, I asked students to reflect upon these questions: (a) Who are your people? (b) What sacrifices did your people make for you to be in this educational experience? (c) What problems plague your people? What problems have their backs against the wall? Once these questions were engaged, I would instruct them to draw a metaphor or simile to depict their people and their current social situation. I chided them not to reduce the complexity of the situation, but to use a metaphor that depicted the complexity. I gave them time to think and draw. Finally, I asked these questions for further reflection and preparation for our semester-long conversation: (a) What kind of leader will you need to become to assist your people and relieve their suffering? (b) What leaders will you join for the thriving of your people?

Using their drawings and prose we created a gallery wall in the classroom. I encouraged them to, for the entirety of the semester, keep their families, churches, neighborhoods at the center of their experience in this degree program. Throughout the course I insisted that they not think generically or individualistically as if they were at school alone or disconnected from the world. Throughout the semester I led them in other learning activities and assignments where they had to continue to consider the specific problems, troubles, challenges, and attributes of their people and ways our study informed those troubles and fostered their leadership formation in their own context.

We do not have the luxury of disconnecting our best minds from the troubles and support of their families and neighborhoods while undertaking higher education. We need healthy models of education that nurture interconnection, understand community, and promote a sense of belonging as a necessity to a healthy society.

FOR REFLECTION . . .

1. "Our lives, our stories, and our realities all intersect with our learning"—Do you agree? Note how you teach at the "intersections."
2. Look back at the questions in the text of this chapter. Consider two or three in a small group discussion.

61

Teach Curiosity

Several years ago, I was expecting a guest speaker in one of my courses. To prepare for the colleague's visit, I asked my students what questions they had for the person. Silence. And not a quizzical silence, just a dead silence. I tried to prime the pump by repeating the guest's research agenda as well as the topics of our course's conversation. The response by students was underwhelming—the not so faint sound of crickets could be heard. I signaled my dismay by using a displeased tone of voice and reminded the students that they must have questions. In distress, a woman blurted out, "I don't have any questions!" I realized she meant that she did not have any deficits. She thought questions only signaled what she was supposed to know but did not. Questions, for her, were a confession of inadequacy, unpreparedness, and ignorance. I had failed to teach that questions were tools of curiosity and a method of inquiry to interact with the guest lecturer.

Since that moment, I have set a teaching intention to cultivate and nurture students' ability to question to express their own curiosity.

In this journey, I have learned that what I am curious about is not necessarily what my students are curious about. I have learned that some students have no curiosity for classroom learning because their energies are tied up in modes of survival, credential earning, and the distractions of family and wage earning. These students are difficult to gather in. I have learned that students have been told that their genuine curiosity is without merit, so they have learned not to voice their real questions or pursue their authentic passions. I have learned that some deep, marvelous curiosity is voiced in a language/vocabulary that is academically unsophisticated, and I have worked to train my ear to hear these curiosities. I have challenged myself to "think like my students" and try to anticipate the kinds of questions and inquiry they will levy toward a reading or learning activity. I want to align with them and use their inquiries as starting points. I have had some success with this tactic—but it's not easy.

Mostly I have learned that students are so eager to please that when I tell them they are to formulate their own genuine curiosity about a topic—they do.

One semester I had two kinds of assignments in my seminar. First, the students were to consider the assigned readings, then, like jazz musicians, riff off the author's argument. I called them Riff Reports. The instructions were to bring to the class a report about what the reading sparked in their thinking and imagination. I challenged them, "Bring your own insights, curiosity—do not repeat the reading, do not report the reading. Consider your own passion, interests, situations, then build, expand, add your voice, perspective, and idiosyncrasies to the conversation." At the beginning of the semester, I modeled in class sessions what I meant by Riff Reports by doing my own version of riffing off the readings. In my three-hour session, I would do a one-hour riff, then two students, each taking thirty minutes, would riff off the same reading. This would give the class three riffs from one reading—a cornucopia of meaning and wonder!

Second, by the end of the semester, the students completed a Curiosity Report, building from the reading, their Riff Reports, my Riff Reports, and the conversations we had in class sessions. The Curiosity Report could culminate in a critical reflection essay, or it could be a creative portrayal. Regardless of its final embodiment (the student's choice), the report had to include a method of inquiry that addressed the student's own curiosity. Students were invited to explain why this curiosity was important to them and their people. They had to sit with the librarian to create a bibliography, interview experts, and go on field trips to visit the locales needed to satisfy their inquiries. By mid-semester, students gave oral reports about their topics, questions, and inquiry methodology. By the end of the semester, students gave an expanded presentation and then handed in a written form.

Watching and helping students formulate their own curiosity was a very different way to teach than telling them what was important, critical, or required in the disciplinary canon. Helping them develop, unearth, and investigate their own agendas was not the same as performing my passions, thoughts, and ideas for them at the front of the class. Witnessing their process of being inspired by our reading, then taking a kernel of their own idea and working it up into a full project, was very meaningful to me. This witnessing gave me a real sense of reverence for their ability to think, create, and hope—I felt as if I was witnessing beauty.

In every case, students selected topics that were personally relevant, intimately related to their life circumstances, and in some cases, life-giving. Our librarian called me to comment on the breadth and uniqueness of their topics and how interested he was to help students who were interested in inquiry. In two instances, I sent students to talk with faculty colleagues whose research interest matched the students. In both instances, the conversations were generative for both student and colleague. Finding like-minded thinkers feels like water in the desert.

At the risk of romanticizing the experience, I did have one student who, in my opinion, got lost in the process. The student preferred being told what to do and how to do it. When that was not the task, the effort needed for discovery and self-motivation was too much. The student was able to articulate a fascinating question of inquiry but could not follow through on investigation and creative research methodology.

Pursuing curiosity requires time for introspection, consideration of ongoing context and conversation, and the wherewithal to investigate. Structuring classrooms for student curiosity seems like a no-brainer, but it has taken me many years to get here.

FOR REFLECTION . . .

1. In your courses, how do you invite students to articulate and learn about their own curiosities?
2. Incorporate assigning students to develop Riff Reports or Curiosity Reports into a course.

62

God Cannot Be Learned

God is unknowable. So, the things of God cannot be learned—they must be revealed.

What does it mean to teach our students to wait for the revelation, to be aware of the revelation, to find joy in the revelation, to trust in the revelation? In what ways might students be better taught to recognize the ubiquitous and concealed revelation? In teaching that which cannot be learned, what is the role of imagination and wonder?

Fortunately, many beloved teachers have journeyed with me throughout my lifetime. Two dear professors are Jack Seymour and Maria Harris. I met Jack in Nashville, Tennessee, while in graduate school. He taught a course whose content miraculously realigned my way of thinking and knowing. In other words, it healed me. The course was Ministry and Imagination. In the course we read the novel *The Clan of the Cave Bear* by Jean M. Auel. This novel is a beautiful story that transports the reader to the dawn of modern human beings and makes privy the lives of peoples who call themselves The Clan of the Cave Bear. Many course sessions were spent discussing the world created by Jean Auel. The final assignment was to think of our own tradition as an unexplored universe, a new world, and in so doing, take a new kind of expedition into that world using imagination as a tool of meaning-making. New doors of thinking about identity, culture, and relationships were opened by the time I completed this assignment. Rather than taking the usual analytical scalpel and pick-axe to look at issues of church and society, Jack challenged us to use our storytelling abilities and artistry to discover what we already knew, but which was yet to be understood. Jack taught me that imagination was not supplementary to ministry, but essential if liberation, transformation, and revelation were to be.

I first met Dr. Harris as a professor in a continuing education program in New York City. I enrolled in her course on imagination and ministry. I have vivid memories of paying as much attention to how Maria taught as I did to the content of her teaching. I remember admiring her audacity of presence and brazenness of speech. She so boldly spoke of God in a way that felt genuine, sturdy, and intimate—all while she was whirling around the room providing life-giving energies. She gave large, deep, and profound answers to questions that, from my hearing, were small and insignificant. She had the patience of a Sufi master. Maria's answers were bedazzled with quotes from literature, contemporary politics, and ancient philosophy. She provided layers and layers of meaning—all seeming to flow through her from a mighty river or a distant star. She, in her freedom, gave to us generously, brilliantly, and lovingly.

Under the guise of imagination, Maria Harris taught me about God. In so doing she said, "Mystery is not that about which you cannot know anything; mystery is that about which you cannot know everything." God is unknowable, mysterious . . . but glimpse-able. You must wait for the revelation—the profound glimpse of God.

On the fourth day of our intensive course Dr. Harris took the class by public transportation to the Cloisters Museum and Gardens in northern Manhattan. We were instructed to bring a sketch pad and pencils. Once at the museum, she encouraged us to look around and get acquainted. After a time, she gathered us back and gave these instructions. She said, "Find some artifact which speaks to you. Once it speaks to you—consider that as an invitation to sketch it. Sit with the artifact; sketch it so you will come to better know it. Then," she went on, "set the sketch aside, linger with the object, and if you have been a hospitable guest, the object will speak to you about important things." She ended her instructions with this command, "Listen deeply." That day I learned that the common, everyday ways of humanity can be tools for mystical encounters of grace and mercy—for those who know how to listen deeply.

Since then, like all teachers, I teach what I know and how I know it. It just so happens that, thanks to Jack and Maria, I know some of the ways of imagination and wonder. It has been my pleasure to teach a course entitled Ministry and Imagination seven times over the last sixteen years. Along with students and with many different co-teachers, I have learned, grown, and had mighty good fun. Together, we have grappled with that which cannot be learned but shall be realized.

FOR REFLECTION . . .

Reflection on teaching is often like meditation and prayer.

1. Name one question that draws you in, with which you grapple on a regular basis.
2. Think about how you feel when you think about / meditate on this question.
3. Think about what draws you in / what sustains you.
    a. Simply take a moment and say thank you for this question.

63

Believe Impossible Things

Alice laughed. "There's no use trying," she said: "one can't believe impossible things."

"I daresay you haven't had much practice," said the Queen. "When I was your age, I always did it for half an hour a day. Why, sometimes I've believed as many as six impossible things before breakfast."

—LEWIS CARROLL, *THROUGH THE LOOKING GLASS*

THE MATTER-OF-FACTNESS OF THE QUEEN'S statement about believing impossible things is her formidable strength. My contribution to a society that must take seriously its issues of inclusion, equity, eradication of poverty, economic justice, and ecological ruin is showing my students that belief in impossible things is their prophetic obligation. I want to teach my students to be more like the Queen, and less like Alice.

The current hegemonic reality would have us believe that the current state of things is all there is. And, how it is now is as it should be—and anything else is impossible. We are distracted from imagining a world of communal mindedness and cooperation. We are taught that justice is impossible, improbable, and, I daresay, imprudent.

For some students, the challenge to believe impossible things is the immediacy of being taught by an African American, female professor who has, by the position she holds in the school, authority over them. "How is it possible," I hear them attempting to reconcile their cognitive dissonance, "that a person deemed by society to be inferior can be in this place of higher education? She must be a credit to her race; she must be an Affirmative Action hire; she must have slept with somebody to get this kind of job."

For other students, the challenge to believe impossible things is when they see someone like themselves—same racial identity, same gender, same hair texture, and possessing the same ability to suck my teeth and roll my eyes like a champ. "How is it possible," I hear them attempting to reconcile their confusion, "that a person like her can be in this place of higher education? She must think she's white. She must have left the church—she can't be Christian. She must be sleeping with somebody to get this kind of job."

If I can press past the immediate narrowness of some students when gazing upon my Black, female body in my own classroom, I am eager to get to deeper urgencies of believing impossible things for social change.

The politics of inferiority, the oppressions of white supremacy, white nationalism, and the current state of misogynoir would have us believe, require us to believe, that the current reality is all that is possible. The status quo truncates the imagination as a way of maintaining control. Unimaginative students routinely resist learning about social transformation and the creativity necessary to disentangle and revision society without systemic oppressions.

Every teacher, if you get to teach long enough, develops a shtick. The word "shtick" comes from the Yiddish language meaning "bit"—as in, a "comedy bit" performed on stage. If you are not sure if you have a shtick or if you are not sure what it is—ask your students; they know. Or attend the annual end-of-the-year skits where students gleefully parody the faculty. Keep in mind that imitation is the greatest flattery and smile during your moments.

One of my many classroom shticks goes like this:

With a wry smile on my face and beginning with a dramatic pause I pose this question:

Which came first—race or racism?

Some students recognize my wry smile, become cautious—suspicious that this is a trick question. Some students hesitate to answer for fear of getting the answer wrong. A silence wafts through the classroom.

I then answer my own question: Racism birthed race and not the other way 'round.

Students' faces signal more suspicion, disbelief, and occasionally . . . curiosity. The silence moves deeper into disbelief and some low-grade fear (like something dangerous is about to happen).

Feeling a teachable moment potentially approaching, I keep going:

It took the depravity of racist hearts to construct race and not the other way 'round. Race was created as a social/political system whose ultimate and exclusive aim is to create a permanent social under-caste of human inferiority.

(Dramatic pause, I breathe deeply so students can breathe also.)

I continue: Given the spiritual evil necessary to maintain the system of patriarchy, white supremacy, and white nationalism, it would make sense to assume that the victims of this social system (all women and children, people of color, the poor, LGBTQ brothers and sisters, disabled folks, for example) should be, and many are, either annihilated, embittered, or paralyzed with fear . . . . Yet, the African American men and women I know, while they have suffered tremendous hardship, oppression, and loss, exemplify a story other than defeat. When you are a people who knows how to believe impossible things, the reality of a situation does not keep you from freedom.

I ask for questions and comments, linger only for a little while, and then continue with discussion questions such as:

- What would it take for you and your people to be able to imagine a more just society—a world without racism, sexism, classism, heterosexism, ableism?
- What obstacles make imagining this society difficult?
- What is at stake for your people if you do not imagine this world?
- What is the role and responsibility of church leadership in the more just society?
- What skills, capacities, and know-how do you need to assist your people in transitioning into a more just society, church, and world?

These are not questions proffering a utopian society, nor are they questions for idle flights of fancy or busy work. Believing in the impossible as well as teaching belief in impossible things is what it will take to save the racists and the victims of racism. If we are to teach our students, in the words of Bishop Desmond Tutu, to endure hardship without becoming hard and to have heartbreak without being broken, then they must have an imagination that can conjure that which evil says is impossible.[1]

FOR REFLECTION . . .

Ask yourself the questions above.

1. Tutu, *No Future Without Forgiveness*, 54.

64

Enchanted Classrooms

In my family's tradition, dreams, visions, symbols, and signs are part of our knowing, understanding, and meaning-making apparatus. I grew up with nightly dinner table conversation that effortlessly included sharing dreams, seeking out interpretations, then the habit of reordering a decision based upon spiritual insight. Our "cloud of witnesses" is a vivid and active part of our spiritual practice. We depend upon prayer, ancestral visitations, angels' interventions, the protection of guides, and warnings by ancestors.

My family's religious and cultural tradition teaches that the world is more enchanted, magical, whimsical, unusual, and unpredictable than typically is made room for by the wider culture's narrow understanding. And since our classrooms are not siloed away from the world—I think that our classrooms, if we would learn to pay attention, are enchanted spaces. Along with this provocative assertion, I want to also say that I do not know, absolutely, what coaxes adult students into learning. I suspect learning, especially for adults, might be dependent upon enchanted happenings in our classrooms.

My grandmother Vyola White Bullock was an elementary school teacher in the early 1900s. My grandmother used to say, "All that is is not visible." She would say this adage is particularly important in understanding our classrooms and in seeking more effective methods of teaching.

If we are to consider the dynamism of the intangible (i.e., enchantment) in our classrooms—what do we pay attention to, respect, and do? In other words, what if more is happening in our classrooms than meets the eye? What if those happenings are more responsible for student learning than we know? What if that which we ignore, or that which we have no knowledge of, is the catalyst for student learning and our successful teaching?

Some teaching is known to open doors, create bridges, inspire students to realize and participate in enchanted endeavors of learning. Equipping students with new ways of meaning-making, allowing students to access ideas of freedom, connecting students' dreaming to actuality and healing can create sparks of intrigue, can create the fire of imagination and wonder that immerses students in new realities. Sometimes, encounters with new knowledges are so palpable that students are moved, literally, into other spaces and other times. My experience as a student, and more recently, my experience as a teacher, has shown me that from time to time, portals open. Some learning causes portals to open, allowing brave enough students to step through. I have seen portals open in classrooms.

As a student, I have, many times, stepped through portals that opened during my study. I was introduced to the work of bell hooks in graduate school. Studying hooks's work was like time travel. I had experiences of remembering what I had not previously known. Learning from hooks's work was a dialogue across the years, across the geographic divide. The first time I read *Sisters of Yam* I felt as if my bone marrow recognized an ancient truth. I was transported into her world, which quickly became our world. I knew what I knew, even more.

As a teacher, I have learned that portals do not always invite us into elegant spaces. Some portals offer struggle, fight, confrontation. A vivid encounter happened while teaching my Introduction to Educational Ministry course some years ago. At the beginning of a lecture in the second session, a student raised her hand—interrupting my lecture. She had a scowl on her face, her lips pursed, shoulders tense with anxiety. Seeing her raised hand, I stopped my lecturing, met her glare with a faint smile, and invited her to speak. She said that she had read the assigned reading by bell hooks from *Teaching to Transgress*. As she spoke, her voice was shrill and loud. She said the reading infuriated her. She said the reading was so maddening that she hurled the book against the wall. Her declaration of angst and anger instantly shifted the mood of the other students in the room to one of caution and concern. I heard one student sigh in impatience, not wanting to give time for this woman to speak her experience of disorientation and pain.

I paused before I answered her. I asked the woman what she had done after throwing the book against the wall.

The student said, "I walked over, picked it up, and kept reading until the end."

I shouted, "YES!"

My shout startled the class. The student's sour expression turned to wide-eyed confusion.

I said, "We must, even if it breaks a hip, wrestle with these ideas until daybreak in hopes of receiving the blessing. And you did that! You wrestled! You went through the portal and wrestled for your blessing!" (This, for Bible reading students, was a recognition that the woman had had the experience like that of Jacob in Gen 32:22–32.) I recognized this student's report as an experience that had taken her into a portal.

From the tradition of my family, this student had been transported and blessed and was telling the story of learning through consternation and dismay. Some portals teach through skirmishes and brawls for understanding and growth.

Portals operate through words and beyond words, with explanations and beyond explanation, with knowledge of the possibilities and beyond our imaginations. Students yearn for vivid experiences that connect them, make them more voiced and more visible. Stepping through the portals provides an immersive experience where the intangible becomes tangible with clarity and needed purpose.

FOR REFLECTION . . .

1. How do teachers recognize when a portal opens for learning?
2. What would it take to plan or choreograph a portal to open for learning?
3. If portals cannot be choreographed, what does it take to coax or summon open the doors of the portal?
4. What kind of teaching stops portals that would open from opening?
5. What do we do that closes the portals prematurely?

65

Teaching Toward and Teaching For

An Invitation

As you think about your teaching and as you look toward the future, think about what you are teaching toward and for. I have offered some beginning suggestions here. I invite you to make your own list.

(1) It is not enough to teach against injustice in its myriad forms of racism, sexism, islamophobia, homophobia, patriarchy, classism, ableism, ant-Semitism, white supremacy, etc. It is not enough to rail against what is wrong and what must be changed, restructured, or done away with.

We, those entrusted with the responsibility of educating, must teach toward, teach visioning, teach futuring. We must teach what we are in favor of, teach what we are for, i.e., the complex notions of community, solidarity, partnerships, coalitions, and collaborations.

(2) We cannot settle for, nor be placated by, that which comes with individualized successful escapes, successful assimilation, successful fleeing into the dark nights, successful trickeries, and moments when one or two outsmart, outwit, outfox, or beat back the oppressors. While that is good, that is not enough. These kinds of successes are illusions and meant to deceive. They come at a high, high price.

(3) In taking up the struggle, fighting, resisting, we must be about more than . . .

swimming against the tide,

standing against the wind,

raising a fist against evil or bullies or the common enemy or fiend.

Resisting. Clenching our fists, fighting, while necessary, keeps us from handling tools and opening our hearts. All these acts-against are, indeed, honorable—but not enough. Our liberation must include acts of vulnerability, creativity, imagination, risky business, and designing for new kinds of hopes for communal living.

(4) We, the collective us—those who are mindful, aware, conscious, faithful, and living as if all lives depend upon all other lives, and all Black lives matter, and that the human family or our earth-house really truly means everyone, all lives matter, and not just a select few who possess all the power and land and clout, and the vote, not to mention all plants, all animals, the seen and unseen that make up the tapestry that is our planetary home—all must understand that passive waiting or simply resisting is not enough. It is foolish to think that we can save just a small percentage of the people and the land and the animals if the rest goes asunder. We are all interconnected. All life affects all other life.

The collective us must teach to understand that all of humanity is intertwined and interrelated, and our survival is threatened by the overwhelming greed and selfishness of a few; so, we must decide to teach what we are in favor of and not just what we are against.

(5) Friends,

Toward what will we teach?

What will we be for? What will we be in favor of, say "aye" to?

What vision will we cast for our community as a common good?

What will we build together?

What will we sacrifice, together, for all our children?

Who will ally, join, partner, pioneer, and experiment?

With whom will we be in solidarity?

We know that what we imagine will happen; that's the nature of imagining.

(6) And if we can, and if we do, make this shift—move from being against to working for that which we are in favor of—then: How will we teach our students to think strategically for what we are for? To mobilize for the new marvelous? To know practices of creativity, healing, dream casting,

imagination, wonder, planning, no longer to combat against, but to use their energies for what we have agreed will be our hopeful future? How will we teach our students to call up from the deep?

What will it mean to teach our students to depend upon their own abundances, knowledges, courages, and hard work? Can they learn to cooperate rather than compete?

(7) Teacher, what do you champion?

I am hoping it is love, compassion, empathy—for all of life—"Lottie, Dottie, and Everybody!" And that you come to believe that life for some does not mean living at the expense of others who have been, for generations, weakened, impoverished, downtrodden, and victimized for the survival and thriving of a few others, selected as special, chosen, or entitled by birthright or muscle or raw greed.

(8) I am hoping we can learn to teach toward justice.

Teach what justice looks like, sounds like, feels like, tastes like, smells like.

Learn to know justice with our intuitions, our inside knowledges that see, smell, taste, hear, or just know because some things are just known.

(9) What kind of study, pilgrimage, lessons do we take to learn how justice lives and breathes and finds meaning and has meaning and is our purpose?

How does justice enflesh itself?

Gather in a circle to talk justice. Resist spending time complaining about the problem of injustice. Instead, dig deeply into what must be made anew, what is needed and necessary. What would it mean to focus the conversation on visioning, dreaming, and futuring? How can we materialize justice? How can we learn, together, to conjure justice?

What if—should we not be able to talk together, vision and dream of our collective future, that then that is why we are stuck?

(10) Knowledge without action is impotence.

(11) Warmongers depend upon our fear. They depend upon our goodhearted willingness to use up our resources in insignificant skirmishes and the business of charity in which no permanent change results.

(12) This is not a question of nuance. I am not splitting hairs between knowing what you are against as opposed to knowing what you are in favor of.

Knowing where NOT TO ride your bicycle is not the same thing as knowing where TO ride your bicycle. The lessons of "no, don't, stop, halt" are not the lessons of "yes, do, proceed, go."

Living in yes takes practice.

(13) You can be against war—but do you know how to work for peace?

You can be against misogyny—but do you know how to love women and our contributions?

You can be against racism—but do you know the cultures, ways, histories, traditions, experiences of BIPOC peoples?

You can be against poverty—but do you know how to create a society without starvation, homelessness, and enough prideful work for all people?

We all have been taught to be anti-Black, even those of us who are Black. Miseducation is just that.

(14) In too many of our classrooms, we are quite adept at training students in deconstruction, negative criticism, dismantling analysis, and scathing critique. How do we train our students in the know-how of construction of ideas, formulation of strategies, creation of newness, in pursuit of the new—regardless of field, discipline, or school?

What would it mean to teach our students to be visionaries, able to converse with one other about the complexities of political identities and agendas, then, together, design the new?

Simplistic thinking is killing us.

(15) Learning to teach toward new visions, new communities, new systems requires different muscles, different thinking, different strategizing, different knowledges than teaching against current injustices and exploitations. This is why it is not enough to be against. Learning the terrains of being-for requires shifted perspectives, new moorings, and emotional maturity to withstand those who thwart the new, the needed, the possible.

(16) Octavia Butler said, "So be it. See to it."

I think she meant us, about our teaching toward justice, and right now.

FOR REFLECTION . . .

1. You have just read sixteen of my concerns/commitments. Take some time. Open a journal. Add two or three of your commitments/concerns. Keep the journal close over the next week. Add others that come to mind.
2. Be mindful that this list reflects the commitments that call you to the next steps, improved teaching, better classroom experiences, healthier school cultures. How will you embody these commitments?

66

Learning to Wait for the Wind

In a society wrought with busyness, contemplation is often deemed a foolish waste of time. Yet, for those of us who want to be reflective practitioners of teaching, contemplation is essential. In considering the needs of students who are navigating our frenetic society, perhaps they, too, need to learn to be more contemplative. Suppose the lessons we teach about social change, eradication of patriarchy and white supremacy, and the need to support the poor into economic stability cannot be grasped or attained without contemplation?

Teaching against the societal values of individualism, violence, greed, and competition needs deep reflection. Raising awareness of the oppressive economic systems, unnecessary suffering, and environmental devastation might mean learning the practices of contemplation if we are to survive. Recognizing the inhumanity of oppressive structures and summoning the creativity to reimagine a society that is more communal, more humane, more equitable takes long periods of thoughtful concentration. Clarity and wisdom can be beckoned through the work of contemplation.

In considering the role of contemplation in teaching and learning, I asked myself if there have been moments in my life when I have had the experience of contemplation from which I might draw to better teach my students. If I am to incorporate contemplation for my own learning, what do I know about contemplation and how have I come to know it? When have I experienced contemplation that was useful? This was the helpful recollection.

My dad had a certain kind of know-how. Among other things, Dad knew the right days to fly kites. This, I have come to understand, is a kind of wisdom. Kite day was not a set date on the calendar. Kite day was the day that Dad knew the wind was just right. How he knew—I still do not know. On the appointed day, usually a spring Saturday, Dad would announce to me and my brother Brent that it was Kite Day. The announcement meant we, in great excitement, would gather the needed elements to build kites. Brent and I would grab previously read newspapers, the stakes used for tomato plants, assorted kinds of string, and old undershirts.

We spread the supplies out on the dining room table, and my father went to work. With the precision of an origami artist, Dad carefully folded the newspaper, attached the stakes into the folds, then, using ripped up T-shirts, fashioned and knotted a tail for each kite. The last step was to apply the string and check the makeshift reeling. Once the kites were assembled, we processed, kites in hand, careful not to drag the tails, to the baseball field across the street from our row house in north Philly. Dad would choose the spot for the kite flying by pausing to feel for the wind. Then, I thought he was just being dramatic. Now, I know feeling for the wind is a necessary aspect of successful kite flying. After quiet moments of wind-testing, we were ready. With great care each kite was placed on the grass and its tail was carefully laid out. My brother and I wanted to run with our kites—demanding them into the sky, but no kite ever obeyed. My father said, "No kite flies from running it into the sky—you must wait for the wind."

Waiting for the wind was not easy because it meant just that—waiting.

What I learned is that once the flurry of assembling the kite is over—kite flying becomes a contemplative sport. Waiting for the wind required patience, stillness, and focus. These moments of waiting were full moments of silence, light conversation, or just observing the surroundings.

With no notice, sometimes gusts would come and abruptly snatch the kite up into the air then just as abruptly slam it down to the ground. If kites became bruised or even destroyed, Dad would fix them or fashion a new one on site. Sometimes, if my brother or I had been lulled into inattention, a gust would take our kite up and the fast-moving string would burn our tender hands. We learned about friction and how to put Band-Aids on fingers. As we became more attuned, Brent and I learned to hold the kite back from flight when the wind was too strong. We learned to judge the right wind and see our kites into lift-off. The moments of lift-off were exciting. Feeling the wind take hold of the kite in a gentle way was the anticipated moment realized. Once lift-off was achieved, the job was, as Dad instructed, to "Keep the nose up!" so the kite would gain altitude and so the line could be let out gradually and evenly. When the kite was ten or twenty feet in the air, the goal was to get the kite to forty or fifty feet. The best flying was when the line was completely let out, and we had time to quietly sit and gaze while it danced, soared, and pranced across the sky. The sky above our field in north Philly was quite a lovely site on kite flying days.

Friends, am I suggesting we all learn to fly kites? Yes! Sometimes the literal is the best. Beyond the literal, I am considering ways of designing learning activities for students, as well as developing practices for teachers, that require time to tarry, linger, be still and quiet. This elegant practice might spawn our best teaching, ever. It might be as simple as breathing and pausing before answering questions in classroom discussion or instructing students to think silently for a few extended moments before asking questions. Slowing the tempo of Q&A might lead to deeper, more insightful inquiry.

Beyond that, crafting exercises that make use of meditation, silence, and stillness to consider complex or emotionally charged concepts could be a refreshing change to the typical patterns of classroom interaction. And of course, for teacher preparation, time spent in silence, in mindfulness practice, and in stillness for re-centering and preparation will likely make us calmer, more present as we teach. The greater change in our classrooms might be developing the sensitivity and patience to wait on the winds of our students, i.e., their curiosity, their questions and concerns, to shape the course and discussions. A contemplative classroom could be a more attuned, a more relevant learning experience.

Let us all find beneficial ways to wait for the wind.

FOR REFLECTION . . .

1. The image "wait for the wind" may be meaningful for you. Others might better engage with phrases like "nourish the soil," or "listen for the spirit." Does one of these connect with you? Or is there another phrase you use to think deeply about the act of contemplation?
2. How do you "wait for the wind" or "listen for the spirit"?
3. What would it mean to your classroom experience to choreograph moments of silence?

Bibliography

Baldwin, James. "As Much Truth as One Can Bear." *New York Times Book Review*, Jan. 14, 1962.

Butler, Octavia E. *Parable of the Sower*. New York: Four Walls Eight Windows, 1993.

Coolidge, Calvin. "Press On!" Address, 1922. In *The Effective Executive*, by Peter F. Drucker. New York: Harper & Row, 1967.

Foster, Charles R. *Educating Congregations: The Future of Christian Education*. Nashville: Abingdon, 1994.

Harding, Rosemarie Freeney, with Rachel Elizabeth Harding. *Remnants: A Memoir of Spirit, Activism, and Mothering*. Durham, NC: Duke University Press, 2015.

hooks, bell. *Teaching to Transgress: Education as the Practice of Freedom*. New York: Routledge, 1994.

Morrison, Toni. "Interview." By Charlie Rose. *The Charlie Rose Show*. Aired on PBS, Apr. 7, 1993.

Morton, Nel. *The Journey Is Home*. Boston: Beacon, 1985.

Murthy, Vivek H. *Our Epidemic of Loneliness and Isolation: The U.S. Surgeon General's Advisory on the Healing Effects of Social Connection and Community*. Washington, DC: Department of Health and Human Services, May 3, 2023.

Schüssler Fiorenza, Elisabeth. *But She Said: Feminist Practices of Biblical Interpretation*. Boston: Beacon, 1992.

Smithsonian National Portrait Gallery. *The Sweat on Their Face: Portraying American Workers*. Exhibition text. Washington, DC, 2017–18.

Thurman, Howard. *The Sound of the Genuine*. Richmond, IN: Friends United, 1955.

Tutu, Desmond. *No Future Without Forgiveness*. New York: Doubleday, 1999.

Walker, Alice. *In Search of Our Mothers' Gardens: Womanist Prose*. San Diego: Harcourt Brace Jovanovich, 1983.

Wimberly, Anne Streaty. *Soul Stories: African American Christian Education*. 2nd ed. Nashville: Abingdon, 2005.

Woodson, Carter G. *The Mis-Education of the Negro*. Washington, DC: Associated Publishers, 1933.

Wooten, Victor L. *The Music Lesson: A Spiritual Search for Growth Through Music*. New York: Berkley, 2008.

Index

www.ingramcontent.com/pod-product-compliance
Lightning Source LLC
LaVergne TN
LVHW100520110826
845146LV00002B/717

* 9 7 9 8 3 8 5 2 6 0 3 3 1 *